£1.29

G000125956

the Education Racket

WHO CARES ABOUT THE CHILDREN?

Duncan Graham

Foreword by Ted Wragg

Neil Wilson Publishing • Glasgow • Scotland

Published by Neil Wilson Publishing Ltd
303a The Pentagon Centre
36 Washington Street
GLASGOW
G3 8AZ
Tel: 0141-221 1117
Fax: 0141-221 5363
E-mail: nwp@cqm.co.uk
http://www.nwp.co.uk/

A catalogue record for this book is available from
the British Library.
ISBN 1-897784-29-5

Typeset in 10/14pt Century Schoolbook by
The Write Stuff, Glasgow
Tel/Fax : 0141-339 8279
E-mail: wilson_i@cqm.co.uk

Printed by WSOY, Finland

For Wendy
and in memory of Fergus and David

Author's Note

Some memories have no doubt been diffused by the passage of time and despite my efforts some inaccuracies will inevitably have crept in. I apologise for these: they have been made in good faith and will, I hope, be forgiven by anyone who spots them. Some geographical and other vaguenesses are quite intentional — there are blushes to be spared, and scents to be confused.

Acronyms

ACC	Association of County Councils (England)
COSLA	Convention of Scottish Local Authorities
DES	Department of Education and Science
	(now Department for Education and Training)
HMI	Her Majesty's Inspectorate of Schools
LEA	Local Education Authority
NALGO	National Association of Local Government Officers *
NCC	National Curriculum Council *
NUPE	National Union of Public Employees *
Ofsted	Office for standards in education
SEAC	Schools' Examination and Assessment Council *

* NCC and SEAC are now united as the SCAA (Schools Curriculum and Assessment Authority) and NALGO and NUPE are now part of UNISON.

Contents

Foreword

Not many people have seen education, during a period of turmoil, as teacher, trainer, administrator, officer, adviser. Duncan Graham has done the lot, from teaching pop singer Lulu when she was a schoolgirl, to advising Kenneth Baker — one end of showbusiness to the other. From Scotland to Suffolk, then Humberside, and finally the National Curriculum Council, he was there.

This well-told story is a pleasure to read. It is both a chronicle and an absorbing narrative. If it were indeed an historical novel, the author would be accused of exaggeration. Could some of the local and national politicians who inhabit these pages really be as cretinous or malevolent as that? They certainly could, and it takes someone with Duncan Graham's professional knowledge, insider experience, and courage, to tell us what really happened.

Some first person accounts portray the writer as a single shining beacon of reason in a sea of ignorance, but Duncan Graham is liberal in his praise of the many public-spirited officials and politicians he worked with during a formidable career. To be successful, education must be a partnership between those who are paid to do a job and those who are elected to check that they fulfil it properly. What a pity that some of the 'racketeers' who emerge in the later stages of Duncan's history of the late 20th century betrayed the high principles of their predecessors and more noble-spirited contemporaries.

Setting up our first-ever national curriculum was a near impossible assignment. No one else could relate, with the same authority, the story of how it was hacked out against the odds. That it is told in well written words, with gusto and good humour, is a bonus. It will be read long after that blissful day when the official papers have all been shredded.

Professor Ted Wragg
Exeter University.

Introduction

BY one of those strange coincidences which so often prove fact stranger than fiction, I spent my first day of full employment having lunch while cruising on the *Queen Mary II*, the famous Clyde steamer on which I had been a student purser, and my last day at work 32 years later lunching on the very same vessel, now moored as a floating restaurant on the Thames Embankment. Quite a lot happened in between as I made my way through the education establishment on both sides of the Border. The further 'up' I went the more I was struck by the decline in care for children and their teachers. In its place was an increasing tendency to treat education as a game for politicians, civil servants, and education experts. Much of what I witnessed was funny, and many of the characters were delightful and eccentric; my enjoyment of it all was only diminished by the dawning realisation that education was and is no more than a racket crossed with a political football.

Fate was to take me from teaching in Dennistoun in Glasgow via teacher training in Ayr to administration in Strathclyde, with everything from the Gorbals to Iona to cope with, and finally to the 'sleepy hollow of Suffolk'. A wider role came my way as Chief Executive in Humberside which included no less than 13 royal visits to organise, and ended after a few years jousting with Prime Ministers Thatcher and Major, and Education Secretaries Ken Baker, John McGregor and Kenneth Clarke.

It is high time to take the lid off, to lift the veil gently and confirm your worst fears, albeit with a chuckle and a wry smile. Perhaps you will then be better able to understand the game and possibly better equipped to deal with it. Take it from me, the future of the nation is certainly not safe in 'their' hands!

Duncan Graham
Appleby, August, 1996.

P A R T   I

Early Days

CHAPTER ONE

Initiation Rites

I tried hard to escape from education as a career, perhaps because both my parents were teachers and finally heads of schools in Glasgow. After a degree in history at the University of Glasgow (which had been fitted in between much more important seasons as a purser on the great turbine and paddle steamers on the Clyde), I was indentured with Kerr, Barrie and Goss, Solicitors in St Vincent Street, Glasgow. The law is a racket too and within three months I was handling 90% of the conveyancing under the eagle-eye of a forbidding lady partner, for the princely sum of £100 a year. I was able to observe at close quarters how old ladies were parted from their inheritances while gratefully leaving legacies to those so adept at fleecing them. It was not for me.

I spent some of my student days when I should have been at Gilmorehill in my father's school, Finnieston Junior Secondary. It was one of the most deprived in a city with few opportunities for inner-city youngsters. A nonconformist and liberal thinker, father had rebelled against the diet of watered-down academic education which was the lot of those who failed the 'quali' (in England the '11-plus'). He turned the curriculum on its head, making the main subjects art, music, technical education and domestic science, with English, maths and science as their handmaidens. He gambled that if youngsters became motivated rather than switched off, they would have to acquire the literacy and numeracy skills to carry out exciting projects. As the 'establishment' reeled in horror, he gathered a staff of talented devoted teachers about him and in no time gurus were coming from far and near to see for themselves the only school in history which was experiencing 'inward truancy' — when staff took the register there were more pupils present than were on the roll! Thousands of youngsters who passed through Finnieston went on to unprecedented success in fields ranging from academia to acting.

At Kerr, Barrie and Goss, one of my duties was to relieve at the switchboard at lunch-time. Any of my secretaries over the years who read this will be able to tell what kind of chaos ensues when I am thus let loose. I cut off a key client or two, and was dressed down severely. However, in the end I did manage to connect myself to Jordanhill Teachers' Training College. Yes, they were so desperate for teachers that I could start training in January, three months late, and virtually on my own. I would have to put in six months to the end of September, allowing for breaks, before being let loose on an unsuspecting profession. Apart from a few weeks of teaching practice in schools, my course had little to do with the realities of survival in the classroom. Masters of method took delight in humiliating students when they came to watch 'crit' lessons and old lags who plainly hadn't been near a school for years gave forth about the theory of education and child psychology which had little to do with training the minipsychopaths roaming the classrooms of Glasgow. Any request for advice on how to quell riots or maintain enough discipline to survive a 40-minute lesson were contemptuously dismissed as being about 'tips for teachers' and much below their notice. I managed in a class of one to fail at religious education, creating the prospect of that department's first ever 100% failure rate. Considerately and tactfully they reduced the pass mark to 35, enabling me to scrape through, and their reputation to remain untarnished. Nowadays they call it norm-referencing.

The gloom was pierced by one Alexander K Powis, Principal Lecturer in History. Seemingly dilettante, attired in a grey suit and suede shoes, red-spotted bow tie with matching handkerchief, he cut a fine figure when visiting the schools in the backstreets of the Gorbals to which he sent me. Urchins were wont to remark on the

colour of his admittedly prominent nose which, they reckoned, resulted from a healthy appetite for spirits. He may have acquired this in
his days as a thespian, relived each year in the superb college pro-
ductions conjured up by James Scotland where he unfailingly brought
the house down.

But he was an inspirational teacher. Even the most difficult classes softened under his gaze, and teachers sitting at the back marvelled
at his mastery of apprentice thugs and ne'er-do-wells. He made history
live and opened my eyes to what real teaching is about. His priorities
were right; lesson one: teaching a class is war — it's either them or
you! Win and you can teach, lose and there's no way back. He sent me
to watch superb practitioners, and then for devilment to Glasgow
High School, where the head of department's teaching technique was
reading round the class. He should have tried that in Finnieston
Junior Secondary.

I spent the months of May to September as Junior Purser on the
Queen Mary II sailing each day from Bridge Wharf at 11am 'doon the
watter' to Rothesay and the Kyles of Bute. I went to the college on
term days at 9am. Invariably nobody cared — or had even arrived. I
did get one note telling me to read Valentine's treatise on psychology
and a paperback on Freud, after which I was deemed to have mastered 'professional studies'. Towards the end of September I received
in the post my Teacher's Secondary Certificate, but I hardly
deserved it.

I was due to take up my appointment in Whitehill Secondary
School just above Duke Street on 30th September, but they didn't
want me until the next day, so I was paid twice for my last trip on
Queen Mary II. By another quirk of fate I took over the timetable of
one Edward Miller who in 1974 was to become the first Director of
Education for Strathclyde and to appoint me as his Senior Depute.

It did not take long to identify the gulf between theory and practice. In all innocence I asked the principal teachers of history and
English for the schemes of work for the years I was called upon to
teach. Supplying these seemed to take them an inordinate amount of
time and when pressed they seemed to look uneasy, even shifty. An
old lag in the male staffroom took pity on me and disclosed that there
were no schemes — in any subject! In English I was faced with a class

of 'low-ability' girls and a pile of dog-eared copies of *Romeo and Juliet*. The girls showed a great ability to discomfit innocent probationers, if little interest in the words of the Bard. In the end we studied the play as a kind of 16th-century Mills and Boon — the blushes were all mine. I like to think it was my success with these lasses that had me transferred to a neighbouring school for a few days to teach a class which included one Marie McLachlan, arrogantly classed as 'less able' by educationists. She was already wowing them at the Dennistoun Palais and as Lulu seems to have done not too badly.

My Higher History class had no less than 57 pupils in it, who rather over-filled the Horsa Hut classroom in which I had the good fortune to teach. At least it was a post-World War II creation. Some colleagues still taught in what had once been a pavilion at Stobhill Hospital for the wounded of the First World War. In my room, those without desks perched on the floor or on cupboards while, clutching my gown about me for security, I cowered behind my high-desk (probably it's now in the museum of education in Scotland Street). In the front row sat the nubile Louise, a gorgeous redhead with luscious blue eyes, who blew kisses to me as I laboured to lay forth about the diplomatic revolution of 1756. No one had fore-warned me about this type of enemy action.

In the other room of this two-classroom unit fully 200 yards from the main building taught one John McKay, a recently-qualified mathematics teacher. At that time so lax seemed his disciplinary control of even first-year pupils that in order to get sufficient peace to cope with my own lot, every ten minutes or so I had to quell his as well. I was relieved when he left for a job in Oban High School, and intrigued when he became a Liberal MP; one way, I suppose, of escaping the horrors of the classroom. In the best political tradition he was soon a Tory. My amusement dissipated somewhat when he became Under-Secretary for Education in Scotland, and without batting an eyelid took to pontificating on teaching and discipline, lecturing the profession on its shortcomings. He is now Lord McKay of Ardbrecknish.

My reputation as a firm disciplinarian came about rather by accident. Amongst the 57 Higher hopefuls was one Rankine, a huge youth who towered menacingly over me and who called the shots with his mates. One fateful day, after I had only just survived the advances of

Louise, young Rankine decided to test my mettle with a direct challenge, based on some whispered but audible allusions to my ancestry and some helpful advice as to where I could stuff my spellbinding discourse on the achievements of Pitt the Younger. Knees knocking I called him forth, pulled my two-prong Lochgelly (deadlier than three) from its 'holster' on my shoulder below the gown, and invited Rankine to cross his hands. After some delay, he complied with overt contempt. I had never drawn the belt in anger, although I had indulged in some target-practice on bits of chalk on the edge of a table. In my ignorance (no lessons on this at Jordanhill) I drew back to the full extent of my golf-swing and let him have it. If I'd missed I'd have cut myself off at the knees, and been done for in the image stakes. Mercifully, it was a palpable hit. Rankine sank to his knees with a low moan and after a recovery period during which the possibility of writs flashed before my eyes, resumed his seat. The word spread and I seldom had to resort again to corporal punishment. George Parsonage, who features regularly in the *Herald* as he fishes bodies from the Clyde for the Humane Society was there that day, and confirmed years later that within an hour, the word had spread across playground, lunchroom and even behind the bike sheds that Graham was not to be messed with.

I don't know if there is any connection, but Rankine in time became a policeman and later trained as a teacher. Some years on when I faced a thousand hostile students at Jordanhill, breaking to them the news that for the first time in 30 years there were no jobs for many of them, a near-riot broke out, and things began to be thrown at the platform. Up leapt Rankine to remind the massed ranks that I was only the messenger, and to hustle me away while still in one piece. I am sure he has turned out to be a superb and dedicated teacher.

There were not too many of those in Whitehill during my spell there. I experienced the first of many insights into the gulf between what we think education is about and what really happens. Male and female staffrooms were strictly segregated. The latter was ruled by Janey Garvan by virtue of having gained a first-class honours degree in the 1930s. Seats were graded in quality to match the pecking order: honours ('Chapter V'), ordinary ('Article 39') and non-graduate to whom Janey seldom deigned to speak. Here was the academic hierarchy which my father had so turned on its head in Finnieston writ large. It's still there in the 1990s when what youngsters need for work — and the lack of it — in the next century plays second fiddle to the 'Golden Age' values of society. I did notice that the more comely lady teachers tended not to be from the blue-stocking brigade.

In the men's staffroom there was not a Protestant work ethic except where it related to the bridge school or to placing bets on Hamilton races. There were more Noon Records than educational journals to be seen. A major preoccupation was opposition to authority and to change. What an eye-opener for a callow dedicated youth to see the lengths to which facts could be twisted to conform with prejudice — a kind of collective lunacy confined to teachers and, as I later learned, university lecturers. Young teachers had a formidable task trying to cope; many succumbed. The few soft seats were reserved for the leading malcontents and left empty even when they were not there. A student-teacher once innocently sat on one, and was frog-marched from the room without his feet touching the floor (or the ghastly litter of milk bottles, mugs and fag-ends which littered it!) Stung by a particularly mingy salary deal, I joined the malcontents and even wrote an inflammatory article for the *Scottish Schoolmaster*, then a polemic rag. Later, as a Director of Education trying to sell change to teachers, I used to imagine myself sitting back in that Whitehill staffroom at the receiving end. It was a salutary way of ensuring that one did not inadvertently pen prose which could all too easily be ridiculed or lampooned.

In odd moments, my new colleagues found time to teach classes and mark essays, but little for preparation or improvement. Once the first year was over and the young teacher had a lesson prepared for every period, he or she could trot this out unchanged for the next 40 years regardless, and on the evidence, many did. 'In-service training' was unheard-of and inspections almost non-existent, apart from that for the 'Parchment' after two years' probation. To add to my rather dubious teaching certificate, I got mine, albeit inadvertently under false pretences.

As I was expounding one day to Rankine and co on the subject of the massacre of Glencoe, Her Majesty's Inspector (HMI) flung open the door of my room and announced loudly that he was here to inspect me for the said parchment. He listened with manifest disapproval to my faltering efforts. The lads played up loyally and splendidly but to no avail. Thrusting me aside, the great man took over the lesson. After ten minutes, he seized the history notebook of a boy in the front row of desks, examined it carefully, mellowed visibly and said 'This is the best ink notebook I have ever seen from the work of a young teacher. Congratulations.' He shook my hand and was gone. I looked in speechless wonder at the book for a few minutes before it dawned on me that it belonged to a boy who had only joined my class that very week! I did not rush after the eminent HMI to confess.

After three happy years in spite of it all in Whitehill, I was summoned by the head to be told that I should apply for a post in my old school, Hutcheson's Boys. Little did I know that James Walker, my Head, and the Rector John Hutchison played golf every Saturday morning when they were not in Cranston's restaurant across from 129 Bath Street plotting the downfall of the Director of Education. Some of the secondary heads in Glasgow with strong Labour links knew more about who was doing what and getting promoted to what than any of the officials in head office. That may explain why the average length of a promotion interview in Glasgow in those days was two minutes.

After a pleasant 15-minute interview at the new school in Beaton Road, I was appointed assistant teacher of history. I was informed that teachers in 'Hutchi' were still paid in cash even in 1962, and can recall queuing up for it in loose change, not even in an envelope, just one month later. I had to forego a special payment of £90 per annum I would have received if I'd stayed at Whitehill!

CHAPTER TWO

Boys' Grammar to Ladies' College

IN Sunset on the Clyde, I recall with affection my days as a pupil attending the old Hutchesons' in the heart of the Gorbals. When I returned as a teacher eight years later much had changed. Most significantly, after 50 years of delay and frustration the school had flitted upmarket. Short of Milngavie or Whitecraigs, Pollokshields was the next best thing. After all the years of expectation, the reality was something of a disappointment. The building was modern and pleasant, but anonymous. It was much harder to feel 300 years of tradition there than in the ancient pile in Crown Street, Gorbals. More significantly, the feeling that the 'lad o' pairts' from slum or suburb was equally welcome was less strong. The fees were no longer £1 10/- a term. The slide towards being just another excellent middle-class school was under way.

I was assigned the classroom next to the staffroom, which came with the most vital job in the entire school — putting the kettle on five minutes before the interval. If I got carried away with, say, the Schleswig-Holstein question, 30 doughty, drouthy men were wont to let me know about it in surprisingly colourful terms — you'd have thought teachers of the classics could have managed words with more than four letters. Some of those who had taught me were still there,

9

not least the head of history whose entire department consisted of me. A born teacher who really brought his subject to life, he told me once that when he returned to teaching after the war, where he had ended up as captain of a destroyer on active service, he had been adjudged by the rector to be too inexperienced to run the school bookstore. Here was an attitude I was to find all too familiar in schools in the years which followed. Experience of the real world counted for less than a canter round the school/university/school closed circuit which narrowed the outlook of so many teachers.

Teaching in a selective boys' school is sheer self-indulgence. In contrast to Whitehill where successes were hard won, here was an institution where the pupils could do it themselves, with minimal help. Broadening their minds was in fact more satisfying than drumming in the facts: they could absorb them like blotting paper. It was essential to be honest with these lads in one's humility — teacher all too often did not know best. The very same inspector who had so generously granted my parchment appeared yet again in my room where the sixth form were studying 'revolutions'. He treated them to a dazzling but condescending overview of Italy's 19th-century Wars of Unification, and when asked diffidently by a bespectacled youth if he was by any chance familiar with the Spanish Civil War, professed a complete mastery. Like piranha fish they stripped him bare. In all decency I slipped out to put the kettle on.

My closest brush with my own Waterloo came in the geography lessons to which I was assigned in sublime and absolute ignorance. Frantic reading of first-year text books the night before each lesson just about kept me a step ahead but all too patently struggling with any questions which arose. At the end of a particularly fraught lesson on gradients and contours, a bright Jewish lad came up to me and admitted he was struggling a bit. He said his dad was willing to pay handsomely for supplementary evening tuition for his son. The thought of extra 'one-to-one' in addition to the frantic mugging up was too hilarious to contemplate. I sacrificed the three guineas an hour and passed him on to the geography department.

At the end of three very happy years, with the additional joys of rugby coaching, and cycling up and down the towpath beside the Clyde at Glasgow Green with a megaphone exhorting rowing fours to break into a sweat, my conscience began to trouble me. The more one takes of the easy end of the market the more difficult it becomes to give up lotus-eating. The desire to change the educational world was proving irresistible. A job was advertised in the newly-opened Craigie College of Education in Ayr which trained primary teachers. It was women-only because at that time men had to be university graduates to teach in primary schools. Boys' grammar school to primary training college for girls was a big step. Not surprisingly I did not make the short leet.

When she failed to fill the post of lecturer in Social Studies first time round, the Principal, the formidable Ethel Rennie, cast the net wider and I was summoned to the presence on a May Saturday morning to face a panel including Sara Cockburn who had successfully made the transition from Hutchesons' Girls in Kingarth Street to the brave new world of Craigie, and who gallantly spoke in support. I was appointed. My father, who had driven me to Ayr, paused with the Triumph 2000 on the way back at a pub in Fenwick to celebrate. Some considerable time later we wove our way across the Fenwick moor on the notorious A77, plastered to the gills. There was no breathalysing then and it was just as well.

I was into a brave new world in every way. A belated attempt was being made to solve Scotland's endemic teacher shortage, which led to new colleges at Hamilton, Callender Park in Falkirk, and Craigie Park beside the racecourse in Ayr. The latter two were mirror-image twins in terms of building, but in ethos Craigie was the real pioneer. The thinking which had led to my father's brave experiments in Finnieston had promoted the view that a diet consisting solely of class-teaching to 40 children, seated motionless in serried ranks facing the teacher, left a lot to be desired, particularly for the less able youngsters. Hutchesons' had taught me that bright pupils can pretty well survive anything educationists can throw at them: not so, the struggling masses. International comparisons were beginning to show our weaknesses — academic excellence rubbed shoulders with the relative failure of at least the lower 60%.

In Craigie the emphasis shifted to individual and group teaching, to learning by doing and understanding, and to enjoying school work. It worked and success was instant. It was as if a great cloud had been lifted from the brows of the young. Imagination was set free, excitement was generated, and motivated children began to self-generate their lessons. To someone who had understood virtually nothing about trigonometry except how to pass exams in it, it was confirmation of a deep suspicion that education had for too long had little to do with childrens' understanding but a lot to do with an easy life for teachers, and with producing an élite to administer an Empire we no longer had.

I have, in the years since, learned nothing to surpass the discoveries of my three seminal years at Craigie. Life was like a perpetual revivalist meeting combined with a 24-hour working day, and in the company of superb, albeit eccentric visionaries.

As you read this with hindsight, your mind must surely leap forward to the later discrediting of the new education of the 1960s. Two things have brought this about, neither of which invalidates the approach. A small minority took things to excess and threw out the baby with the bath water. Nothing we did at Craigie suggested that schools should abandon tables, long division and grammar, or mastering the basics of literacy and numeracy, or give up completely the teaching of whole classes at the appropriate time. But somehow the value of motivation through enjoyment of success rather than the depression of failure was distorted until anything not instantly enjoyable was 'wrong' — no trace was left of 'learning until it hurts'. As you will discover when we reach the national curriculum, the rot had spread widely, particularly in England. The fault lay in the excess, not in the theory. The theory I heard from one expert in the 1980s that infants could learn to read simply by handling books could not be laid at our door. Who could believe that if exposed to books children would teach themselves to hold them the right way up, learn to distinguish pictures from text and in time learn to read! Give me the 'Janet and John' approach every time. It was the perpetrator of this rubbish who, when asked by the mother of a five-year-old if her child would be safe in her school, replied 'Don't worry, we have here a self-disciplining community of five-year-olds.' The mother wisely took her infant elsewhere.

The introduction of the 'project' method, whereby work in every subject was devoted to a topic such as 'The Vikings' or 'Life in France', was an initial success. Subjects became related as never before. Young children do not have minds split into compartments labelled, history, geography, science, and so on — these are adult concepts and convenient devices. Inevitably this approach too was taken to excess until continuity was lost or, worse still, hapless children got 'Vikings' year after year until they'd had more than enough. In a school in Argyll years later, after a class had 'done' penguins for a month — life-cycle, habitat, polar regions, poems about them, pictures of them, you name it, they'd done it — one child when asked for a final essay wrote simply 'This project taught me more about penguins than I wanted to know'!

The other thing which went wrong was that these excesses, untypical though they were and overshadowed by the great benefits brought to children, became embroiled in a political battleground. Blithely ignoring the evident shortcomings of traditional teaching, the right wing mounted a 'back to basics' campaign, which was based on misconception and sentimentality. There is nothing more potent than Golden-Ageism and a longing for what 'we' had at school — that is if you are middle-class and intelligent, and probably educated privately. Playing on legitimate worries about the exceptions which hit the tabloid headlines, the right attacked the method rather than the errors in its application. As a result, instead of starting from children's needs and seeking balance, we have had the customary British 'yah boo' approach with woolly liberals on one side and the 'back to high stools and quill pens' dinosaurs on the other. The heat thus generated has not created much light for pupils and teachers or done much to raise standards; it may have depressed them. It has certainly depressed me.

There was plenty of fun to be had at an all-girls' college in the mid-1960s. This was the age of the miniskirt and until one became used to it, the central gardens on a summer's day could be quite compelling. The pleasure palled with close proximity to no less than 900 ladies, but a favourite ploy was to walk visiting male luminaries through their midst while plying them with abstruse questions on education theory. Some of the distracted comments this brought forth were as revealing as the scenery. While on the whole male staff resisted the temptations with professional restraint, there were exceptions, and not a few went 'down the drive' as Ethel Rennie termed it. Some of the ladies were not above provocation, although the vast majority, not least the 'mature students' (women over 30), were wonderful, talented and hard-working.

My innocence of extra-curricular activities was illustrated on the evening when a colleague with a yacht invited me for a sail into the sunset from Ayr harbour. Arriving at his mooring I was surprised to find the president of the Student's Council already, and fetchingly, aboard. We cleared the harbour, shaped a course for Holy Island 11 miles away and I was given the tiller. A surprising degree of confidence in my embryonic ability was soon expressed and the rest of the crew descended to the cabin to make tea, closing the hatch a few minutes later 'because of down-draughts'. We were just about to hit the aforementioned Holy Island when they finally emerged, a little ruffled, with a strong mug of tea for the helmsman. Perhaps that's why I took up sailing and in due course owned my own boats on the Clyde: in succession a Loch Long, a Hunter Europa, and a magnificent Contessa 26 which I named *Charisma*.

Hector, my running-mate in the Social Studies department was a tram buff. He measured time with his Aberdeen City trams' pocket watch, poked his fire with a Glasgow Corporation points-changing implement and owned his own tram at the tramway museum at Crich in Derbyshire, which he visited most weekends with his devoted wife Leo. I hold her in the highest esteem in the 'greater love hath no woman' category. On arriving at Crich she would don her authentic Glasgow Tramways cleaner's overalls, and proceed to launder Hector's tram! Live up to that ladies, if you can!

Our head of department, Derek Davis, a garrulous southerner, was a master of the indiscreet. On one occasion he regaled the maiden ladies of the staffroom with intimate details of an embarrassing ailment of the testicles which had affected him, and later reassured a lady recovering from goitre that her 'eyes didn't stick out half so badly now'! At the other end of the spectrum was the urbane head of religious education. Like the lilies of the field he toiled not, neither did he spin, but he stopped late each evening until 7.30pm, reading his *Glasgow Herald* and dozing. He then called ostentatiously on the Principal to wish her goodnight and arrived home when his poor wife had fed, watered and bedded three young children. She then served him a three-course dinner.

I doubt if he deceived Ethel Rennie for one minute. After years of ribbing in the common-room at Jordanhill, she seemed understandably determined to get her own back. Her powers of invective and scorn, and her razor-sharp wit made her a formidable exponent of the put-down. At a meeting of her board of studies, of which I was the most junior member, I can recall the day when she altered, I believe deliberately, every word of a beautifully composed draft letter by Jack Tosh, the Head of English. In a moment of lunacy when she asked for final comments, I asked her why she had left the 'Yours sincerely' intact. Her wrath then was only matched on the day when, as she watched from her room (a kind of ship's bridge from which to spy), I backed the college's brand-new minibus into the front of her equally new Triumph Toledo with the resultant expensive noises widely reported by bystanders. The most terrifying thing was that she was able to transfix me at 50 paces, helpless like a rabbit caught in the headlamps. She never once referred to the incident — she didn't need to.

I had other disasters that she didn't know about — or did she? There was, for example, the day I perorated for 20 minutes on the 19th-century Radicals to 20 lasses, before I worked out that the state of my flies was of more immediate interest to them. I slunk behind my desk trying to keep a straight face as I repaired the damage. So flustered was I that I then inadvertently transposed the initial letters of the names of the Radicals Cobbett and Hunt. Not many lectures to students conclude with a round of applause. I achieved much the same effect when I sat on the model of Crossraguel Abbey which the college technician had just taken three weeks to make for our first ever TV lesson.

The most enjoyable part of my job was visiting the little schools of Ayrshire and Wigton to assess students who were undergoing the dread 'crit' lesson before my eagle eye. A favourite ploy for these set pieces was to find an exhibit — often a stuffed animal from the Kilmarnock museum. There was an owl called Oscar who made more farewell appearances than Frank Sinatra. I regret bitterly advising a large 'awfy genteel' girl from a nice family not to resort to Oscar. To my horror she proceeded instead to hand out drums and cymbals to a class of veteran six-year-olds in a school in downtown Irvine and gradually lost control despite her polite pleas for attention. Mayhem ensued. Lecturers were supposed to intervene only in extremis. I felt moved to when a precocious little gangster got the student's beautiful head between the cymbals, and another began rattling her knees with a drum stick. Order was only restored after a few cuffs behind the ear hole from me of the type which would land a teacher in court today. The student took my well-meant advice and became a librarian in the Doon Valley.

It was a pupil in the same class who, when I was watching him counting with Cuisenaire's rods, turned to me and said, 'Hi Jimmy, where's the red bugger?' Compared to him, coping with the little girl in obvious discomfort who slipped me a note which read 'I have dun the tolyet on mi desk' was child's play. Whenever secondary teachers complain how difficult it is to teach sixth formers, I have a quiet laugh and raise a symbolic glass to the real heroes of education — the ladies who turn unruly gangs of five-year-olds into numerate and literate little citizens. Ethel, who believed in practising before preaching, made me teach a reception class in Tarbolton for a full autumn term. I took to bed on Christmas Eve, and barely woke up for Hogmanay.

These were glorious years for me. I was learning and helping to shape and improve the education of Scottish youngsters, in one of the few institutions where their needs and requirements were put above self-interest. While I learned from Ethel Rennie some things not to do, I witnessed at first hand what vision and determination can achieve. I saw too how important image is. Craigie was pristine in maintenance and decor. Harbison the head janitor, immaculate in grey uniform, greeted every visitor at the door and put each one at ease. The gardens blossomed in ordered profusion. The scones were home-baked, the filter coffee served in bone china and the common room, in contrast to Whitehill, was a mug-free zone.

The trouble was it was not the place where most change could be effected by a man with a mission. A few more years of luxuriating in the four months summer vocation, marred only by the return of the students to spoil the staff seminars and the coffee-time debates, and I could never have brought myself to leave. I consoled myself with the thought that some day I might become principal of a training college, and in the meantime applied for the post of Assistant Director of Education in my native Renfrewshire. Although Ethel made her views on educational administration clear — 'prostituting your talents' was, I recall, the phrase — she gave me her reluctant blessing. Soon there were so few colleges left, that there would be none for me to come back to, even if I'd wished.

PART II

Renfrewshire and Strathclyde

CHAPTER THREE

Assistant Director of Education

THE post in Renfrewshire came by accident. Hugh Fairlie, the Director of Education, had decided to regularise the position of Ian Halliday, at that time merely seconded to head office in Glasgow Road, Paisley. The rest of the list were there to make up the numbers. Apparently I so impressed the councillors that they made the 'wrong' choice. Hugh in those days seldom lost out to his committee and the compromise was that he took both of us. That explained how when I first arrived, and not for the last time in my career, I had no room to call my own. Later a tiny room was carved out of the ladies' loo, but the partitions left something to be desired. I was privy, if that's the word, to sounds and confidences which on the whole I could have done without. Ian had a cracking room with a huge double desk and oak panelling.

A job had to be created for me and instead of starting off with supplies, stores, welfare, school meals and bus passes — the lot of most apprentice administrators — I was given the task of creating from scratch a youth service and the first ever teacher's in-service training centres in Scotland. Both remits gave scope for pioneering and learning.

Fortunately, the county had just acquired in Eddie Taylor one of the country's best youth officers. I am deeply in his debt for broadening my perceptions of what education is about. Academic work in schools is only part, albeit an important one, of it. For some youngsters, occupying their spare time constructively is equally crucial to their development as citizens. Youth workers with their less formal approach can reach many who are beyond the scope of formal schooling. In Renfrew, which had virtually no youth clubs, the way forward lay in youth wings attached to schools. They could draw in youngsters still at school, support them during the day and at weekends, and give them continuity when they left.

I had a bitter lesson to learn: most of the old-guard heads did not want this kind of thing in their schools — first-name terms, no corporal punishment, leaders without degrees, discussion rather than instruction — where would it all end? We had a battle royal to get any co-operation until we appointed leaders at depute-head level with powers to manage the whole school after 4pm and grant public access, overruling the head if necessary. The interest of young folks and indeed adults seemed at times as nothing compared to the vested interests of the heads. We had to 'take' equipment such as tools, cookers, and footballs away from them and 'lend' them back to make the point that schools were 'ours' and not 'theirs'. Since then many community schools have worked well in everyone's interests, and thank God not as in one school where a white line down the middle of a corridor separated 'school' from 'youth'. I suppose the best of back-handed compliments came from the chief constable who later said that juvenile crime had dropped since youth wings had been introduced.

There was a similar reaction from schools to the opening of the brand-new outdoor centre at Ardentinny. The aim was to give every pupil aged 15 a week away from home to mix with others, to learn about the countryside, and to sample a range of outdoor activities from sailing and canoeing to orienteering and camping. It was not an 'Outward Bound' experience; there was no intention of terrifying or testing by ordeal. Most of our 15-year-olds had never been away from their parents for a break, still less learning to live with and tolerate others. Thousands who read this book will testify to the success of David Lilley and his staff in enriching their lives and extending their horizons — more than 47,000 at the last count.

Heads doubted if pupils could spare a week from their school work. Some tried to opt-out of the scheme, showing scant regard for the real needs of their pupils. However, when the school year in Scotland, co-incidentally, was shortened by a week there was not a single protest and the extra week's holiday was accepted without complaint.

Things got really out of hand when the rector of Greenock High School, came 'o'er the hill to Ardentinny' (in the words of Harry Lauder's song), and started swinging his Lochgelly in the boys' dorms. He was expelled by David Lilley like a miscreant schoolboy caught in the act. A huge towering dominie (who, with his lanky depute, was known inevitably to the pupils as 'Fat Man and Robin'), his pet hate was 'the permissive society'. In his time he flogged boys because their hair was too long, and later because they were skinheads. A religious man, he meant well but seemed to pay little heed to the need to make allowances for the rebelliousness of youth. He could only skin cats one way.

We took all the secondary heads to Ardentinny for a week, after which we had no further troubles. What the excellence of the instruction failed to remedy, the nights in the bar of the Ardentinny Hotel soon put right. Lo and behold, the exam results went up instead of down. How sad that a quarter of a century later Ardentinny's future hangs by a thread due to 'economies' (the euphemism for cuts). What was that about the price of everything and the value of nothing?

I was cutting my apprentice teeth on the less attractive side of the education establishment. In-service training proved no less difficult. We deliberately chose not redundant schools but pleasant houses for the centres — Priory Park in Paisley and Glenpark in Greenock. Both were equipped to make teachers feel prized and esteemed, with comfortable lounges and teabars. Christine and Rose who managed them did all in their considerable powers to put visitors at their ease. Although the curriculum was seething with change, hardly a teacher came voluntarily — apparently none of them needed help. This was a remarkable commentary on attitudes, based on a 'king or queen in the classroom' attitude, and quite alien to what was going on in other jobs and professions. So in-service training had to be compulsory at first. Later the flood-gates opened. People began to admit to inadequacy and insecurity, and, like the Windmill theatre, we virtually never closed. Soon what was looked upon askance in pioneering Renfrewshire had become the national norm, to everyone's benefit, most of all the pupils'.

Another task which invariably fell to me was addressing womens' guilds and womens' institutes when they were hard up for a speaker. My first-ever foray to such a meeting still makes me blush 30 years later. The venue was a church hall in Houston, Renfrewshire; the topic (chosen with malice a' forethought by Hugh Fairlie!) was 'My vision of comprehensive education in the 1970s'. My preparation was meticulous and the end-product would have passed muster as a PhD thesis. On my arrival I was greeted by 19 ladies surrounded by 100 empty seats. Five were knitting furiously, three fully engrossed in their crochet, two were breast-feeding infants and the plucky remainder (including the chairman) were soon asleep. Quite a few woke up for the hymn and prayer which came after it had all ground to a premature halt. And everyone was quite 'with it' when the tea and scones arrived. A silver collection was taken, including my half-crown; I was reminded of the similar occasion when the chairman counted the takings and announced, 'You have been so generous we will be able to afford a better speaker next month.'

Over the years I addressed handfuls in village halls, 500 from the pulpit of Exeter Cathedral and thousands in halls from Bradford to San Francisco. I even won applause from 600 Womens' Institute stalwarts in the Sparrow's Nest theatre in Lowestoft. I never forgot the lesson of Houston — a successful speaker must tailor his material to his audience. If he can make them laugh, intentionally that is, so much the better.

I then had more than enough work to keep me going, but sufficient time to sit at the feet of the master in manipulating committees of elected members. In Renfrewshire, although some members sported party labels, most were independents at heart, more interested in 'their' schools than in party dogma. Good-natured rivalry between Greenock and Paisley was stronger than that between Tory and Labour. Many belonged to that sadly vanishing breed, those devoted to good works. One such was Mrs Young, 84 years of age, but chairing a committee with all the enthusiasm of a youngster and willing to go to any lengths, provided that she got her hearty lunch at 1 o'clock prompt. Committee meetings were so timed that lunch had to be provided. Hugh Fairlie used this to advantage, filling in the two hours before lunch with innocuous items, and slipping in the meaty ones he didn't want debated at too much length at two minutes to one when tummies were starting to rumble. On one occasion we ran out of trivia at twenty past twelve. Quick as a flash Hugh was on his feet confiding that he didn't know whether the filing cabinets at the new St Columba's High should be grey or green. After a furious debate, green carried the day by 15 votes to 13 at ten past one. They then approved unanimously an increase in the budget of £2 million and were having their soup and rolls by 1.14pm. Incidentally, a new councillor, a Lithgow of the shipping family, proposed that all meetings could be over in one morning each week well before lunchtime. He failed to get a seconder!

Perhaps Hugh's greatest triumph came over his passion for golf at Pitlochry. Tall and lissome with a swing as sweet as that of Bobby Jones, with plus-fours to match, he devoted much energy to ensuring his handicap remained at four. With a conference at Pitlochry most weekends, it was his custom to mention casually the next one to committee, and seek their formal approval. It was so painless that it seldom registered with them. However, one day Davie Miller, the ex-miner whom we all loved to hate for the abuse he heaped indiscriminately on officer and fellow member alike, heaved his vast bulk upwards, moving the table forward three feet as he did so, and fixing Hugh with a baleful eye bellowed 'Hey there, Director, we canna just ha'e you gallivanting aff whenever you fancy. I move we refuse permission.'

Routine forgotten, the chamber came to life and all eyes switched to Hugh. Ever so slowly he rose to his feet and turned to the chairman.

'Sir', he said, 'ex-provost Miller has made me the happiest of men. At last I shall have a weekend free for my wife and children whom I seldom see as I toil night and day in your service.'

'Wait a minute, Director' says Davie, sensing defeat but not sure why, 'If we tell you tae go to a bloody conference, then you'll go tae a bloody conference!'

Hugh tossed his clubs in the boot and off he went, with the added justification of a man whose committee forced him to work at weekends. Magnificent.

It was my unenviable lot to have to accompany Davie Miller to conferences from time to time. The ordeal started when he levered himself into your car. He would hang his 18 stones from the door until the hinges creaked and groaned in protest. On arrival at Crieff or Pitlochry, Davie would order the first measure of his unique beverage — a double Haig in a glass of milk. The mere sight of it was enough to turn a delicate stomach. But that was only the start. Before he made for the luncheon or dinner table, I had to get hold of the head waiter and explain that Davie would go through the entire menu — sampling all the starters from brown Windsor to paté, followed by all the entrées and in due course the spotted dick and the scotch trifle. All would be washed down with copious draughts of Haig and milk. It gave a whole new meaning to 'à la carte'. Awed waiters used to hang about in clusters to witness the gastronomic prowess of our man. Fortunately there were fewer choices on offer then than now. After dinner Davie liked to dance. Like many a hefty soul, he was light on his feet, but chose his partners indiscriminately, despite whatever protests they unavailingly made. I am led to believe that King Farouk did the same. Davie could clear a ballroom of ladies without any bother at all. I gather that the whisky and milk started as a device for surviving temperance meetings, rather in the way that Gladstone had pure gin in his glass during his marathon budget speeches in the House.

I learned from Hugh Fairlie the art, and that's what it is, of working with a committee of elected councillors. He taught me never to underestimate their corporate common sense, even if some like Davie looked as thick as two planks. It was Davie who brought me to my knees by spotting the flaw in a case I was putting for more youth leaders. 'Awa hame, laddie, and do your homework. Ye'll ha'e a better chance next month, then.'

I remembered this when I went to address the Town Council in Port Glasgow. Round the table were 14 wee men, each with a flat cap on. I only just made it through the debate led by ex-Provost Tommy Stanton, a real character even at 70. He had just contrived to have the council pay for the reception following his wedding to a local lady of

25

mature years. At the preceding nuptial mass, I felt it was a bit unfeeling of the priest to bang on so much about the true purpose of marriage being procreation. Port Glasgow was en-fête and well lubricated, Tommy was conveyed straight from the reception to the school prizegiving where, after revealing that he had 'devoted a lifetime to propagating the youth of Port Glasgow', he exhorted the assembled pupils 'no' to get carried awa' and 'aye to keep their feet on terracotta.' It was he, when I entered a meeting late, who explained to his colleagues that I 'was a busy man, delayed by his nefarious duties'! I hope he meant 'onerous'.

They don't make 'em nowadays like Tommy or indeed ex-Provost White (they'd all been provosts [mayors] at least once). You always knew when White was about to speak in committee because he took out his teeth, cleaned them, and popped them back in just as he rose to speak. Although there was no drink at lunch — in contrast to the City of Glasgow as I later found — White brought his own carry-out, with the result that he was prone to dropping off soon after the afternoon business started. An unobtrusive snooze is one thing, a disgusting rasping snore which shook the room and ended with a loud snort is quite another. One day the chairman, Robby Robertson, had had enough. He proposed that Councillor White be expelled from the chamber with immediate effect. Deep down beneath the snoring, something stirred, some awareness of procedure permeated the fuddled head, and rising briskly, teeth uncleansed, White said loudly, 'I'll second that!'

He was out before his feet could touch the ground.

Something irreplaceable has gone from local government. There seems to be no room for the Whites and Stantons, the Davie Millers, and their ilk. Collectively they cared and served their communities well with little reward. Their successors attend to the briefing from Central Office or Walworth Road, and then do what their whips tell them. How sad! I treasure to this day the sight of Mrs Young, middle-class and polished, arm-in-arm with Mrs Martin, Provost of Greenock and of humble origin effortlessly crossing the political and social divides as they set off to press the secretary of state for more cash for 'their' schools. I contrast that with the fate of my chairman in Suffolk, Felicity Cowley, of whom more later, who was reviled and then sacked by her own group for refusing to countenance the dismissal of infant teachers to meet government cost limits. Local government has little power today other than to obey orders, and has attracted to it many elected members who seem to care little about services, and more about their own advancement. Is it too late to restore the balance? In England there could soon be nobody between central government and 24,000 individual schools to speak for parents and community. It is slowly dawning upon us that the 1960s were halcyon days of improvement in services and full employment. Who would argue that things are better now than then?

The officers who served in those days were also more colourful and confident. It is dangerous to be a 'character' now with politicians who prefer grey non-entities — apparatchiks rather than innovators and improvers. Men like Hugh Fairlie and Stewart MacIntosh in Scotland and Alec Clegg in England would not survive long in their posts today. The combination of their professional advice with wise political leadership has been destroyed to the great loss of society. For a youngster like me in the 1960s, it was a wonderful experience to sit at the feet of the great Directors of Scotland, like Macdonald of Inverness, and Young of Perthshire who once sliced a golf-ball through the gym window of his school in Pitlochry and had to go round, apologise to the head, and ask for his ball back.

Renfrewshire had its share of characters amongst its officers. Archie Sinclair, the Depute Director, lived in apparent chaos and presided over teacher staffing from an office piled high with papers and cardboard boxes, all of the latter being transferred ostentatiously to the boot of his Jaguar each evening, giving the impression of hours of toil at home. Of course they never left the boot until he returned to work next morning. Caught speeding by the police, the chief constable let him off provided he went round primary schools giving a road safety talk, accompanied by a large 'Tufty' doll. Tufty adorned the back seat of his car for months — better by far to have paid the £20 fine, with no licence points to lose in those days. Ian Ross, an austere Catholic, had a weakness for miniature cameras on which he spent the housekeeping money and more. He once came into my room, thrust a tiny Leica into my hand and said 'Please give me that.' I did and he explained that he could truthfully tell his wife he had been given it. He had, I think, been educated by the Jesuits.

One of the most remarkable was Douglas Binnie. He was as handsome as an ex-Spitfire pilot should be. Every time Douglas made for his car, he went through a complete cockpit drill right down to checking the tyres and the lights. He was not a man to be with if you were in a hurry. Devoted to his mother, he had girlfriends but never a consummation, licit or not, as ex-girlfriends were wont to testify. Weekends away tended to be platonic rather than action-packed, they implied. His mother passed away when he was in his 60s and he married a domestic science teacher to compensate.

It fell to Douglas to lead the 1969 British India school cruise to the Baltic aboard the *Nevasa*, with myself as his assistant. It came to be known as the Porn Cruise. The sixth-form lads not unnaturally paid a visit or two to the sex shops of Copenhagen, and brought a load of magazines back for their mates' delectation. When one of these slipped from under a pillow at Douglas's feet he was outraged. Ignoring my pleas that lads would be lads and that Nelson had turned a blind eye, Douglas went on a porn-hunt and soon had three sacks of the stuff. While I assisted the ships' officers to dispose of it, checking it meticulously to confirm that it was as bad as was feared, word reached the inevitable tabloid reporter who was enjoying his cruise. He cabled the story to his editor and ensured a lively reception for the *Nevasa* on docking at Greenock. Some rotten swine tipped off Customs that the jazz-records Douglas had bought in Sweden and which had no labels were pornographic too! They held him for three hours until they got hold of a gramophone. By that time we had news that the teachers posted missing in the Tivoli gardens had been found. Not one of the 900 pupils contrived to get lost, which surely tells us something.

My time as assistant director was drawing to a close. Archie Sinclair, after years of trying, had got himself promoted to Director of Education in West Lothian and there was a vacancy for Depute Director . Sizing up the competition, I took the chairman's advice to toss my hat into the ring. Hugh Fairlie was not amused.

CHAPTER FOUR

The Greasy Pole

THE post of senior depute — ie number two in the hierarchy of officers — was the first promoted post I'd applied for, after nine years in
education. It was very nearly the last. 'Let the best man win', had
seemed the attitude appropriate to lobbing my hat in the ring. A furious Hugh Fairlie disillusioned me in no uncertain terms. If he'd told
me he'd set his heart on Ian Halliday I might have backed down — at
least that would have been honest. Instead he contrasted my lack of
experience with all three other assistant directors, and said that ability was no substitute for years at the coal-face. Even I wasn't so daft
as to fall for that — Binnie and Ross for two were hardly world-class
administrators, and Halliday, while hugely competent, like all of us
had his weaknesses. Nonetheless, but for chairman Robbie
Robertson's encouragement, I might have betrayed my convictions
and withdrawn.

While the post was being advertised and formalities gone through,
I saw another side of a man I had so much admired — if his judgement was sound what had he to fear at the interviews? I was packed
off to lead a cruise on the *Uganda* to Madeira and Lisbon and found
that when I went aboard, I was not to sit at the captain's table — the
cruise equivalent of the kiss of death. An interview with the captain
revealed that head office had decreed it. Just imagine the board of a
major shipping company meeting gravely to ordain which assistant

directors would not sit at high table! Oddly they seemed to have agreed that chairman Robbie, who had decided to go at the last minute, should sit there. Later I was to hear junior civil servants when challenged over trivia claim that the decision was not theirs but 'the Minister's'. It is easy to blame them up there. The captain had been nobbled, but by whom?

It was a good cruise, after the pettiness had been left behind at Customs House Quay in Greenock. I recall that our arrival in Madeira was unfortunately timed. We disembarked a party including several hundred teenage girls two hours before HMS *Tiger* arrived with half-a-thousand sex-starved marines from the Arabian Gulf. Liaisons of what we frantically hoped would be of an unproductive nature were numerous and teachers sped frantically around disentangling where they could. I remember approaching a sixth-former from Eastwood in the embrace of a husky marine with a polite request to disengage.

'Fuck off,' he said.

I did.

It was more than enough to keep one's mind off the plotting at home. Two days of acute seasickness prolonged by an injudicious BI curry before we reached Lisbon had a similar effect.

With a bit of luck, Fairlie need not have had to worry about my prospects. The dormitories on *Uganda* were converted from a labyrinth of former mess decks dating back to its troopship days, with half-landing stairs set within the main ones. One evening after dinner at the captain's table, and having used my rank shamelessly to dance with all the prettiest young lady teachers in our party, I made for my customary pre-turning-in inspection of the boys' dorms. In the third one I only just had time to marvel at how frilly the lads' pyjamas seemed to be when the heavy hand of the marshal-at-arms descended on my shoulder.

'I am the cruise-leader,' I explained.

'And I'm Adolph Hitler,' he responded.

Fortunately I wasn't the first to have made the same mistake and it all ended in laughter. Just as well the tabloid reporter chose the Baltic cruise.

All good things come to an end, and the ordeal loomed ahead.

Interviews were conducted in those days like mass inquisitions, candidates facing the full 32 members of the Education Committee. I came through the winner but Fairlie persuaded a committee, plainly reluctant to thwart their own director, to interview Halliday and myself again. In the interim, groups of tame heads wrote saying they wanted Halliday. Subject Inspectors whom I'd persuaded to break sweat for the first time in the teachers' centres, doubted through a deputation to the chairman whether I had the experience. They might not, they hinted, be able to work with me. Fairlie called me in to say I was a dead man if I got the job — he'd have to work round me. Jeffrey Archer would have been disbelieved if he'd written a novel about it. On the day of judgement, despite the behind-the-scenes plotting, the vote for my appointment was overwhelming. To his eternal credit Ian Halliday was the first to shake my hand. It was two uncomfortable years before the director handsomely admitted he'd got it wrong, but by that time, sadly, he'd lost the confidence of his committee and his reputation was tarnished. What a lesson for the future that was. Every time a chief officer goes to the limit with his committee and loses, he does himself irreparable damage.

I took over teacher staffing with great trepidation — I too had been fooled by Archie Sinclair's boxes-home-in-the-boot routine! Gordon Brittan, the chief clerk, and I commandeered a skip into which we threw every paper in Archie's room bar the personal files. We were never queried about a single one of them. Years later in Suffolk when my personal assistant took to filing almost everything in the bin, I took comfort from what had happened in Paisley.

The biggest problem in staffing was simply shortage of teachers, particularly in less popular areas like Greenock, and in Catholic schools. In one school with both handicaps there was not one qualified teacher of English and had not been for ten years or more. 'Uncertificated' teachers were the only expedient to keep schools going — if they were able to draw breath and vaccinated they were in. Even so, schools had to resort to part-time education with pupils being sent home in rotation. In St Stephen's in Port Glasgow things were made worse by the fact that the head himself was effectively part-time. Charlie Harkins ran several dance bands in his spare time, fronting on trumpet himself his famous Kit-Kat Band. He had had an extra phone installed on his desk which I once managed to pick up in his absence to find a local club requesting a booking. I don't know who was the more surprised when I told them who I was.

Standards in this school were abysmal: I once lost my temper and demanded changes to the timetable or else. Charlie had on the wall one of those fancy ones with little lego-like bits to stick in a grid. We improved it to my satisfaction — little did I know that it was a 'front' for gullible people like me. The real one, quite unaffected, resided in his depute's room. Charlie would sit behind his desk whenever I called, chubby face aglow, forehead a-sweat like Louis Armstrong, doing his trumpet-finger exercises under the desk until I gave up and went away. I'm sure he cared about the children, but only after the bands were fully booked.

We made valiant efforts to attract teachers with all sorts of inducements, especially to students when we did our milk-round of the colleges each year. It was a waste of time trying to entice them from Aberdeen or Edinburgh, even with flats and living allowances as bait. We recruited in Canada and more successfully in Northern Ireland where the troubles had by now started. Our best ploy came with the introduction of guidance teachers in Scottish schools. We jumped the gun and advertised before the scheme was formally approved and pinched teachers from all our neighbours. Oddly they all happened to teach technical subjects, science or mathematics, the scarcest subjects. All we were doing was to redistribute the West of Scotland's shortages. When I took over staffing in Strathclyde I had to move some of them back out of Renfrew.

From Strathclyde I was to lead a hunting foray to Boston. We held court in a hotel there after advertising our presence. Curious teachers came from all over the States — even by car from California. They were attracted by our lack of violence in schools, deterred by the salary levels, and astounded to find that you could teach for 40 years in the UK without ever having to go on a retraining course, or sit a formal examination. Years later I was to remember this. In the end 200 excellent teachers came over, most to return but some to settle in Scotland. Some came because of the climate — I suppose all things are relative. In Boston when we were there, you risked frostbite running between hotel and drugstore for breakfast, unless well wrapped up. When we got back to Prestwick we were questioned by the press on how much it had cost, not on how many teachers we had recruited. We invited the press to meet the first batch of 50 recruits when they flew in, but only the *Ayrshire Post* turned up.

I paid a visit to Greece in the midst of my staffing woes and in a sense came to envy their system whereby teachers are centrally directed to where they are required. Promotions are unsought and come in the shape of a directive which might take a man 200 miles from his family, to be allowed home only once a year. I created a near-riot in a Greek staffroom when I showed them a copy of the *Times Educational Supplement* — the vast section of advertisements it contained blew their minds. They could not believe that teachers here could pick and choose what they applied for. Bits of TES were being torn out as souvenirs when I left, no doubt to be marvelled over in neighbouring schools. Incidentally, they had a real national curriculum in Greece and no messing. There was one set text book per subject, and the same lessons were taught to each age group in each subject on each day in each school. Mysteriously they had no discipline problems. They had no equipment either. I watched a lesson on calculators supported by a blackboard drawing of what one looked like; even the teacher had never actually seen one.

It was one thing to recruit teachers, it was another to deal with their peccadilloes. As with all social groups the county's teaching force contained a large number of conscientious and hard-working professionals whom one seldom met, and a small number who caused all the trouble. The interests of pupils had to come first; and after that came trying to saving those in trouble from themselves and often from disgrace. There is little to be gained from depriving a wife and children of a livelihood, by throwing the book at someone. For example the 35-year-old primary head, a Rotarian and pillar of society, who had fallen madly in love with a nine-year-old blonde whom he confessed with unconscious irony he was teaching to play the organ, was quietly found a job as an insurance salesman. The science master and art mistress found *in flagrante delicto* among the test-tubes by the janitor got references carefully-worded enough to start a new life together in New Zealand: it was after hours, there were no child witnesses and perhaps the janitor might have looked the other way.

A marvellous pair were the staff of the two-teacher school at Langbank. Man and wife, they had not exchanged a word in school or out for several years. As I sat with the wife in the staffroom on one occasion, husband came in and pinned a note to the board which read 'Staff should note that school will close at 3.30pm today (Friday).' Parents complained about a lack of communication which was not resolved by marriage guidance counsellors but in the end by a threat to fire them both unless they could work together in school at least.

The inveterate swearer in front of pupils cured himself — some would say a miracle cure. Having invited himself to join me on the first tee at Kilmacolm Golf Club, we became a threesome when a small rotund figure with a cherubic face, only partly obscured by a baseball cap, joined us. I introduced the newcomer as Bishop McGill. As we traversed the fairways, expletives poured from the lips of our teacher friend, and the still air rang with select profanities. At the fourth green he turned to our portly companion and said, 'That's a hell of a funny first name you have Bish.'

'I am Stephen McGill, Bishop of this diocese,' he replied, 'and I believe that for the time being you teach in one of my schools.'

No more was said, or indeed needed to be said.

There were sad stories too, of those who had taken advantage of children, and those who were alleged to have and where proof was lacking. These were days long before the prominence and emphasis given to child abuse today, but those accused had to go if there was the slightest suspicion. Help could only be given after they had been dismissed. Sometimes the trouble came from psychiatrists and doctors who placed the interest of their patients before those of children. I can recall vividly the classics teacher at a Johnstone high school who had to go to a mental institution because he was given to kicking those children who annoyed him — and there were many. His bearded consultant, who on closer scrutiny turned out to have been the eccentric of my class at school, sent him back with the heartening news that he was likely to assault fewer than before his partial cure: he needed back to see how he would get on!

Saddest of all for me was the primary head who retired full of honour after a distinguished career. His erstwhile number two went to a junior officer of the authority accusing him of taking some books on antiques from the school library before he left. Instead of a tactful enquiry as to whether, by any chance, the former head had kept them accidentally, my junior went straight to the police. Sergeant Plod interviewed him with a view to prosecution for the theft of goods to the value of £32 in the shape of books. Two days later the former head's body was washed ashore near Girvan. Which of us is so self-righteous that we can treat our fellow man so unfeelingly?

Problems relating to pupils also came my way and all too often they seemed to concern clashes over the trivia rather than the basics of education — long hair, short hair, failure to wear uniforms. Expulsions were rare, in marked contrast to today when many thousands of pupils are permanently excluded from schools each year. Clearly some children are ungovernable but fewer than you might think. More often schools find it convenient to be rid of, rather than to cope with them. Nowadays there are no obvious courts of appeal and public opinion sides too readily with schools. But what of entitlement to education? What of going the extra mile? I don't believe that children are so much more badly behaved than they were 30 years ago. I do believe that education authorities then played a vital role in ensuring fair play. The pupil expelled from Greenock Academy for advocating that the school play football instead of rugby was returned to the fold, as was the girl at John Neilson High School in Paisley excluded because her trench-coat was the wrong shade of navy blue. This school had on its staff the celebrated W Steele Brownlie of the Scottish Schoolmasters' Association, who rose at dawn each day to pen a letter to the *Glasgow Herald* about the outrageous treatment of teachers. He was much less concerned about pupils, such as the four-foot-eight-inch boy from the slums of Ferguslie Park whom he and colleagues refused to teach because he had allegedly punched a six-foot-three-inch gym teacher — presumably in the knee. The case collapsed in laughter all round when both appeared before an education committee. The most violent and disruptive have to go of course, but not the ones whose faces simply do not fit, or who might depress the school's ranking in the league tables.

Life was exhilarating in the early 1970s. In stark contrast to today new schools were replacing old to the tune of a dozen or so in Renfrewshire alone each year. Pupil numbers were still growing and expansion was in the air. There was sufficient money to maintain and improve services and Renfrewshire's reputation for quality was high. Complaints from parents were few — even when schools were closed without the endless consultation which takes place today before it is decided not to close them after all. The director and his staff in most of the 33 authorities in Scotland were respected professionals, working in partnership with elected members. There was a genuine partnership between local and national government, with respect for their complementary roles — truly a national service locally administered.

I met senior civil servants for the first time at this stage of my career, and even Secretaries of State. In those days they received deputations hospitably, listened — or at least appeared to — and occasionally gave ground. The contrast between the atmosphere at a meeting then with Jack Maclay or Michael Noble and Kenneth Clarke in the 1990s is too extreme to contemplate. In my professional lifetime we were then as close to putting the needs of children first and treating education as a privilege rather than a burden, as we were ever to be. I can't help thinking that politicians in the 1970s set a better example to the youngsters they exhort to behave than do their present-day counterparts. Blaming everybody else, lying through one's back teeth, and condoning sleaze were not in fashion 20 years ago. I do recall that the occasional politician even resigned when found out.

But the storm clouds were gathering. There was a growing realisation that, with the 1960s' dip in the birth rate thanks to the pill, expansion would turn to decline — a process notoriously difficult to manage. Pundits were forecasting a long-term downturn in the economy while it was becoming fashionable to attack the profligacy of public spending. Corporate management was the 'in' buzzword and accountancy-led management was in vogue. From that time stemmed the practice of cash-limiting budgets instead of assessing real needs. Today's cancelled operations and NHS waiting lists are the inevitable result.

Change was coming and it was capped by the news that the government intended to reform the shape of local government. This was bad news for the Director of Education in Peebles who had six schools in his care and ran the book on who would become the next Director of Education in authorities from Wigtown to Shetland. It was to be much worse for those of us in the West of Scotland. To create a strategically viable river-based region, Strathclyde was to be created, engulfing not just Renfrew but Argyll, Dumbarton, Glasgow, Ayrshire and Lanarkshire as well. This would create a mammoth conglomerate with a population of some two-and-a-half million — 50% of Scotland's population, stretching from Kilmarnock to Coll. It seemed pretty crazy at the time and still does, although splitting it into 12 parts in 1996 seemed a bit of an over-correction. Even more baffling was why a Tory government would want to hand a permanent Labour majority control over areas at least two of which, if left alone, would remain Tory strongholds. Robbie Robertson led an intelligent campaign against the creation of the monster, but in vain. In 1974 the end of civilisation as we knew it would see the demise of Renfrewshire. While the administration of education in potentially the largest local authority in Europe would furnish something of a challenge, much more interesting was the question of who would get the plum jobs. Norman Buchan the Labour ex-minister and a local MP thoughtfully dropped in to Paisley to tell us in no uncertain terms it would not be us. It was rather like that lottery finger in reverse. Our consolation was that as he left in his car with a few choice comments ringing in his ears, he drove his car smack into the side of a passing bus. We looked down on a little man who was literally hopping-mad. The bus driver didn't seem to be any too thrilled either. I wonder if the incident made it into one of Norman's celebrated folk-songs.

CHAPTER FIVE

The Strathclyde Mafia

STRATHCLYDE was born in a welter of politics. Its sheer size and potential to challenge the Scottish Office made that inevitable. So too did the coming together of the Labour leaders of so many of the old authorities. In the jousting for position on the greasy pole that is politics Dick Stewart, an ex-miner from Lanarkshire, came to the top — a real Tammany Hall operator if ever there was one. He was ruthless and he had to be — Labour held so many seats that there was every prospect of infighting between factions. Stewart's power over colleagues was awesome. Transgressors emerged from his office shaking and pale, the butt of threat and coruscating invective. A party machine soon emerged which took us from paternalism and informality to whipped voting on even the most minor issue. As a consequence real debate no longer took place in committee. It was all buttoned up in group meetings. Unless an officer was willing to take the risk of attending these, he had little chance of influencing decisions. The pressure was on to produce papers which 'suited' politicians and suppressed problems or drawbacks. Openness was at growing risk from that day.

The councillors had to make adjustments in other ways. The early 1970s had seen the rise and fall of T Dan Smith and Poulson and the imprisonment of George Pottinger, a civil servant who fell off the fence on the wrong side. He had the difficult task of staying close to

Hugh Fraser in an effort to persuade him to finance the Aviemore complex. Strathclyde had to be cleaner than clean which meant even rejecting any bottles of whisky or calendars presented at Christmas. Many of the councillors, particularly in Lanarkshire, had enjoyed a spot of what had seemed harmless enough to them, but was now on the wrong side of the line. They were plainly bewildered at the outlawing of the customary backhanders and favours. A few went to jail along with Lanarkshire's former County Architect who had embarassingly become the top man in Strathclyde.

In looking for chief officers for the various departments from education to highways and finance, new confidential criteria were drawn up. There were to be no more 'cult' directors, administrators known to the public for their views, who might appear as rivals to the newly power-hungry politicians. Suddenly it was no longer healthy to be professionally well-known; appearances in press or broadcasting were out. Grey men with compliant views as anonymous as Whitehall mandarins were in demand. Too blind to sense the change and to conform at least until appointed, the great men of education continued to enhance their public personas. John McEwan of Lanarkshire, our own Hugh Fairlie and Jim Wallace of Ayrshire looked forward to a brisk contest. Wiser men such as Andrew Cameron of Dumbarton retired. In spite of, or because of, their brilliance, their success, their dedication to education, they were swept aside, humiliated. Jobs at a senior level were carved up and allotted to political leaders of the former authorities to fill. Glasgow's former politicians could, in effect, nominate the director of education, Lanarkshire's the regional architect and so on until all the top posts were filled. This was doubly unfortunate. Not only had Stewart MacIntosh of Glasgow, one of the best directors of education Scotland has ever produced, retired, his most obvious successor David Adams was killed in a car crash. From a distinctly third-tier position came Edward Miller in his early 40s, and adjudged grey and 'safe'. It was an enormous jump for a man who was a first-class administrator, but who seemed overtly surprised to be there. He was not a leader in the Fairlie or McEwan mould. He was to be tested to near-destruction by the forces which came to bear on him. No wonder he took to returning to his room to remain incommunicado for a couple of hours each lunchtime — not for him the canteen or the pub lunch with colleagues. It was agreed that the post of senior depute to Eddie would be a key appointment, but who was to fill it? The great men were not interested and said so. A few would linger on at divisional offices in their former areas — humiliation enough — but no way at HQ. I was sure it was not going to be me. Whatever talents I might have had — or not had — Renfrewshire had been labelled 'Tory': the kiss of death.

I felt I had to go through the motions of applying and was duly summoned to the city chambers to make up the numbers. Labour friends from Paisley told me that I ought to get the job on merit, but could forget it! This was cheering confirmation of how the carve-up was going — the former Lanark council was rumoured to be 'due' this post. The good Lord intervened in the shape of a bus strike in Easterhouse. Would you believe it, a critical mass of Labour panellists were too late in arriving to vote — even though the whole thing was held up for an hour in a vain attempt to get them there. I scraped home by a single vote. Robbie Robertson, leader of the Tory rump on the new council had rallied the rest. I like to think that justice had been done. Eddie Miller seemed surprised but not displeased. The blue train taking me back to Whitecraigs broke down and I sat in agony for over an hour, unaware of the outcome.

Now there were two of us at the top, and a new chairman in Bill Harley, a friendly man who painted scenery for STV and was struggling to survive with the Stewart mafia. Excitement and terror alternated in rapid succession as we set up base-camp in 25 Bothwell Street, formerly Glasgow's further education office. I had a pleasant bay window two storeys up on the corner with Wellington Street.

Our new masters ranged from a few of the old guard who cared about schools to a powerful majority to whom education was just another empire to be fought over. Bill Harley was very clearly junior to the chair of the new policy committee who called the shots and saw education as a 'milch cow' to be raided for resources for other purposes. Eddie Miller was no longer in sole charge of running his department but a member of a corporate management team chaired by a powerful chief executive, Lawrence Boyle. The great traditional empire of education in local government — by far the biggest of the services — was fragmented with finance, transport, building, and staff other than teachers passing from our control. We only just kept control of the teaching force. If there were gains, as was claimed, in this brave new world — efficiency, economy, close co-operation with other services — they were in my view quite eclipsed by the loss of concern for schools and children. We became too busy with the 'game' to have much time for the front-line players. We lost touch with schools. If there was trouble in one, whereas in the old authorities we would have known the background and personalities, we now had to look it up on a map, work out a route to get there and hope for the best.

The unions had an enormous influence in Strathclyde — principally those for manual workers and white-collar staff: NUPE and NALGO (now part of Unison). They had great influence with members, to the extent that at negotiating meetings councillors and union leaders alike used to turn on officers as the common enemy! One had constantly to remind members it was their policies which were causing the disputes. With the closed shop Eddie and I had to join NALGO and were soon called out on a one-day strike. We refused to desert the schools and were within an ace of expulsion and dismissal before common sense reasserted itself and we were given exemptions on the grounds that legally someone had to mind the shop.

Teachers' unions were much more naive and relative child's play for the council. Idealists with a grouse are always easier to deal with than hard realists with a bottom line. Teachers' leaders invariably opened meetings with a discourse on how they worked harder than anyone else, which went down a treat! They sure knew how to lose goodwill. As with so many in education in the 1970s, they were oblivious to the real issues. Callaghan's 'Ruskin' speech in 1976 had won great support with its theme that the nation was losing confidence in education. Educational success was now vital to the economy. We were 'failing' over standards as tables of comparison with other countries seemed to show all too clearly. The publicity given to liberal excesses consequent upon the changes of the 1960s had left people worried and insecure. The 'secret garden' of education now appeared more impenetrable than ever. One of the main reasons why these concerns were not addressed in time and which led to the national curriculum debate in the 1980s was that on both sides of the Border local government reform had left education fighting the wrong battles for the wrong reasons. The IMF funding crises and the 'Ruskin' speech should have been taken more seriously. In the words of Richard Crossman 'the party was over'.

Against this background, by some miracle, education in Strathclyde came to work reasonably effectively. I was responsible for staffing, troubleshooting (there was plenty) and the day-to-day running of the service. We set up six divisions based on the former authorities, and devolved as much power as we could to these. It was found impractical to run several thousand schools from HQ — a point for government in England today to bear in mind where they seem keen to manage 24,000 of them from Whitehall. Confidence was gradually restored, but it was hard to have much contact with schools. The Strathclyde PR machine sent out a brochure 'introducing' us to schools. I later saw the picture in it of myself pinned to a staffroom wall with a dart through the eye! I escaped from HQ when I could — especially to Argyll as you will discover in a later chapter — but was nearly always called back on some pretext or other, even from Edinburgh where I was now beginning to cut my teeth on the national scene.

I found myself as professional adviser to both COSLA (Convention of Scottish Local Authorities) at their meetings in the capital and to the Scottish Teachers' Salaries Committee. Later I was to hold similar posts in England with the Association of County Councils and with the Burnham Committee, which had 80 representatives on each side and met interminably to hear set posturings in seedy London hotel ballrooms — the only rooms big enough to hold them.

In Scotland things were more practical and civilised, with only about 16 present. It helped that there was one really big union, the Educational Institute for Scotland (EIS). In my day the teachers' side was led by one Keir Bloomer, a brilliant hard-headed negotiator and a descendant of Keir Hardie, the Scottish socialist revolutionary. When the full group had pushed things as far as they could, and the civil servants had laid down the limits of what could be paid for, Keir and I were sent off to slug it out in private. Over dinner we had the sharpest intellectual jousts I have ever experienced, with no holds barred. More than once our prandial deals averted strike action in schools and kept the paymasters content too. On one occasion I recall telling Keir he was 'wasted' in a union! Was it my fault, I wonder, that the poacher turned gamekeeper when some years later he became a distinguished education officer in Glasgow?

Politics at national level tended to be more civilised in the 1970s than they are now, with more give and take. Labour were in power and the Under-Secretary for Education was one Frank McElhone. Frank struggled manfully to cope. Simple sentences and monosyllabic words were the ones for him. He had a heart of gold and an empathy for deprived children which I have not seen matched, and no one could question where his priorities lay. His dogged persistence in the House of Commons, had once led Margaret Thatcher to dismiss him in exasperation as 'that MacElhone' with the final 'e' pronounced. Whenever he came to Strathclyde he was a joy to talk to. His civil ser-vants cosseted and protected him. On the public platform they pled with him to stick to the script prepared for him. When he didn't, they would melt away from the hall, unable to contemplate the conse-quences. He and I shared a platform in Dundee in November 1977 when he decided to go for it. His attack on obscenity was tactfully described by the *Glasgow Herald* as a 'personal and at times emo-tional address'! To him, as far as we could gather, obscenity was not page three of the *Sun* but selling children short in the classroom. Sir Keith Joseph or Ken Baker might have put it more elegantly, but not with such conviction. I wonder if Michael Forsyth has the same deep concerns about what is arguably even more of an obscenity today.

A constant feature of life in Strathclyde was coping with the reli-gious divide. Forty per cent of our pupils attended Catholic schools, administered by the authority, but in co-operation with the Archdiocese of Glasgow and the able and diplomatic Archbishop (now Cardinal) Winning. Mercifully lacking the violence of Northern Ireland, similar tensions existed in the West of Scotland, with much prejudice on both sides. For many years the first question asked on meeting a stranger tended to be 'What school did you go to?' All job-application forms had a prominent section for 'Religion' and it was not unknown for what was entered there to influence the filling of posts. Tom McCool, a brilliant education administrator, who took over my post in Renfrew in 1970, very nearly lost out on religious grounds alone. What a loss that would have been.

I made it a priority to work with the Catholic authorities and was blessed to have the full support of Monsignor Coyle, the church representative on the Education Committee. He combined this heavy responsibility with a full-time post as parish priest in Blackhill, one of the most deprived districts in Glasgow, when he could easily have made education his full-time remit. It has been my privilege to meet with no finer man than Frank. Like Winning he knew a good malt when he saw one, and the three of us used to sip a prime Glenlivet from the Archbishop's exquisite crystal goblets as we wrestled with the consequences of prejudice. Winning was deeply aware of the conservative nature of his flock but open to progress too. We tried to have a combined Protestant/Catholic primary school on the same site with shared dining and playground facilities. What a wonderful way to break prejudice at a time when no Catholic could play for Rangers and mixed marriages were frowned upon by priests. I'd like to say it was a success but sadly we ended up with a partition in the middle of the dining room and a 'Berlin Wall' in the playground. It takes a lot to change 100 years of prejudice. Some Orange leaders considered me 'suspect'; of being too friendly with the enemy. I like to think it has got better since then; certainly, in that respect it was a relief to move on to Suffolk in 1979 where no one ever asked what your religion was or even cared two hoots.

Frank Coyle and I attended together the opening of a new school in the Motherwell area — a ceremony I shall never forget. It was one of the stormiest January nights imaginable. The organisation of such events now lay with the region's PR team headed by the inexhaustible Harry Dutch. They managed to arrange the platform party on a dais in the gym in a mirror-image of what they had intended. My attempt to point this out was rejected as interference. The local councillor acting as chairman blithely introduced the chief constable as a lady JP, myself as Father Coyle, and the head of the school as a social worker. He paid a particularly warm tribute to the architects and builders for all their sterling efforts. At the end of the proceedings a small boy presented a basket of flowers to a man while at the other end an angelic little girl offered a box of cigars to a rather embarrassed lady. At this point there was a horrendous gust of wind and a corner of the roof lifted off, showering the audience with debris. Fortunately no one was hurt but there was nevertheless more than one inquest held the next morning.

School openings and speech days are not my favourite events. At openings all the credit goes to councillors and politicians who have had no hand in the process but make all the noise, fighting over their place on the platform from which to extol their achievements. It was ever thus and there is more satisfaction from doing a job well than in taking credit for it. I can recall the day when Norman Buchan insisted on opening a small school in Erskine and kicked up hell afterwards because the stage had been too small to find room for his wife, Janey, now an MEP. I took malicious pleasure in reminding him that he had claimed the achievement as his and that he should have designed a bigger stage.

Speech days are worse. I can remember as a pupil myself enduring old buffers giving forth with inspirational words when all I wanted was the summer holidays to begin. Now that I am the old buffer, I try to make it as short and humorous as possible. The shortest one I ever managed was at Kilmarnock Academy. I was down for a ten-minute address but the local toastmaster who was acting as chairman took 25 minutes of rhetorical wizardry to introduce me, ending with the challenge 'I've heard our guest today is one of the best speakers in the West of Scotland. Now is his chance to prove it!' I stood up and burst out laughing. The teachers, parents and youngsters roared with me. When the merriment subsided I sat down without a word to the loudest round of applause I have ever received.

Strathclyde provided the best of experience for surviving everything life could throw at one. I never again was to face any crisis which I had not seen the likes of before. Unfortunately the job tended to put me more in the limelight than the new breed of politicians relished. While I had no ambitions to be a prima donna, I was finding it equally hard to be grey. Stewart MacIntosh, the former rugby internationalist who was director in Glasgow in my father's day, was, with Hugh Fairlie (warts and all), my role model. Both put children, schools and teachers first. Stewart could visit a school, address teachers by name, and even ask the janitor how his wife was getting on after her operation. Whether it was a superb memory or an excellent filing system no one ever found out, but staff worshipped him and would do anything for him. He knew when to use discretion too. On one occasion my father stole away from Finnieston to watch a mid-week afternoon match at Hampden. Two rows away sat Stewart MacIntosh. Apparently they raised bowler hats to each other in silent acknowledgement. No further reference was made to magisterial truancy. This kind of thing was no longer 'on' in the 1970s. I had to have quiet words with Bob Crampsey and Archie McPherson, both heads whose work with the BBC as sports commentators was difficult to overlook on a few too many Wednesday afternoons.

In Renfrewshire Hugh Fairlie had been known to every teacher and was always there in sympathy and support in time of trouble as well as joy. The vast anonymity of Strathclyde made me long more and more for a manageable 'patch of my own'. In Scotland there were likely to be few of these. On a fateful trip to Sicily I learned from English colleagues that there were still some 'Renfrewshires' left south of the border where a man could make his mark.

The visit to Palermo was an interesting one. You could tell at a glance which schools were mafia-sponsored: resplendent, rich, well-equipped — and which were not: dilapidated, squalid, neglected. Here was a novel way to allocate resources. The mayor had decided to take them on. Not only was he surrounded by a dozen bodyguards with ominous bulges under their tuxedos, but there were tanks parked around the courthouse, where one or two of Cosa Nostra were on trial. He told me that what had inspired him to risk his life (I think they got him later) was the inequalities in the schools. Like Frank McElhone he knew where his priorities lay but the Godfather he had to contend with was more formidable even than Dick Stewart.

CHAPTER SIX

Lord of the Isles

STRATHCLYDE had its compensations. For me the best of them was that it included Argyll and the islands. It's writ ran from the Gorbals to Iona. When the region was set up, its inception was greeted with even less rapture in Argyll and Bute than elsewhere — they were underwhelmed. But there was a subtle undercurrent. The canny natives knew that the previous authorities had been so impoverished that provision of both buildings and adequate numbers of staff had been poor. There was a backlog due to lack of resources. Playing their cards the right way with 'Big Brother' could pay handsome dividends. And it has. No fair-minded inhabitant could deny that, from new schools and libraries to bus and ferry-passes, Strathclyde has done them proud. The only black mark lies against the Highways Department. Those wonderful new roads built in the 1950s and 60s which opened up the Cowal, Loch Fyneside and brought the scenic highway to Tighnabruaich, have been allowed to reach a shameful state of 'shreds and patches' and the roads in the towns look like patchwork quilts. One wonders what foreign visitors make of the rocky road to Oban — from Tyndrum to Taynuilt, from Connel to Oban, disconsolate groups of privatised roadmen haunch and patch where they should be replacing and up-grading.

In 1974 these roads were at their peak, and I for one was determined to use them. Those who have read *Sunset on the Clyde* will

47

recall that much of my early life had been spent in Argyll and the isles, from the day when I was 'evacuated' to the Cowal Temperance Hotel in the East Bay of Dunoon in 1940, via my youthful summers at Corrie in Arran, to my days as assistant purser on the steamers of the Clyde. Shortly after my appointment as Senior Depute Director of Education, it was confirmed that I should have day-to-day responsibility for the six geographical divisions of the region. Not by chance, Dunoon was my first port-of-call. I had crossed from Gourock by car-ferry — the days when as a child I had watched a dozen and more turbines and paddle-steamers call at the pier before 10am were long gone. I walked round past the dis-used coal-pier along the front to the Cowal Hotel. The days of temperance hotels had passed and it was now the Education Offices for the Argyll and Bute Division. Externally it looked much the same, and I imagined Rory the chauffeur easing the Arrol Johnston to the front door to drop off affluent and abstinent guests, with their trunks and hampers. I peered through the former dining-room windows only to see rows of filing-cabinets and clerks scurrying about where once waiters in bow-ties and tails had held sway. For a moment I thought of the one occasion when the prohibition had lapsed, to permit the holding of Sir Harry Lauder's Silver Wedding celebration. By next morning not a sign or trace of alcohol remained.

Inside much had changed, the grandeur supplanted by bureaucratic austerity. But a surprise was in store. As I was ushered into the office of the Divisional Education Officer, the aptly-named Charles Edward Stewart, I realised that this was the very room which my aunt, when proprietor, had used as her splendid bedroom-cum-sitting-room on the first floor with splendid views across to the Cloch Lighthouse. In the days when not even the poshest of hotels had 'ensuite' facilities, it had sported a rather splendid wash-hand basin. In 1974 it was still there, an incongruous survivor in an otherwise spartan office. Charles must have wondered what sort of oddball had been wished upon him, prepared as he was for a formal briefing, but instead faced with my preoccupation with the plumbing.

I recall promising him every support in his efforts to improve the lot of the pupils of Argyll. With what must have seemed to him to have been suspicious alacrity, I accepted his invitation to see for myself and to join him in a tour of inspection. This was the first of many visits. In the years that followed, every excuse was exploited, particularly if it occurred in May and June. Locals referred to Strathclyde officials, with some justification, as 'Mayflies', too delicate for the winter winds and storms, but seen swarming in great numbers in the summer months. In truth, such were the pressures of life at HQ, that a few days 'lost' in Argyll on legitimate business was a justifiable compensation for the hard days' toil in Ferguslie Park or Shotts. Argyll was important in other ways too. In a region of two-and-a-half-million souls, people could all too easily become ciphers, mere statistics. Despite its vastness only 90,000 folks lived in Argyll, and one could begin to see them as individuals, and to recognise their strengths and weaknesses, their problems and their aspirations. I remember little of the characters of the rest of Strathclyde, not because they didn't exist — far from it — but because one was defeated by sheer numbers.

In the early years of Strathclyde, travel to the islands for officials was by car and ferry, and there was time to spend with people, and if the winds blew, there was every chance of being marooned on Coll or Tiree, genuinely unable to respond to the calls from HQ. I once had three 'extra' days on Tiree which I shall never forget. Apart from having time to make serious inroads on the gantry of 180 malts in the local hotel, with the willing assistance of Tiree teachers, I was more able to appreciate the problems facing a tiny secondary school and the desperate desire of the population to keep their youngsters on the island as long as possible. Those who left for the hostels in Oban or Dunoon at the age of 12 were those who found it most difficult to come back as young adults. Later I was able to persuade councillors to invest in secondary schools such as that in Tiree, which they might simply have closed as unviable. Mark you, that was not the main preoccupation in island minds, as the gales whistled about us and the *Columba* remained stormbound in Oban.

The chief constable had decided in his wisdom to give island policemen a spell in Glasgow, and city men a tour in the outback. A new constable had arrived in Tiree — young, keen, ambitious, a stickler for the regulations. This was awkward. There were perhaps 20 vehicles on the island, many of them in an extremely battered condition, partly due to the fact that when, for whatever reason, they fell off the road they were hauled out of the ditches and the machair by passing tractors. The more obvious bashes were ironed out, and normal service resumed. In no time at all, the new policeman had booked several of the islanders for drunk-driving, an offence never before heard of in these parts. Feelings ran high, and there were dark rumours of insurrection. To add fuel to the flames, and well into his stride, the new man began to demand sight of MOTs, a document not in everyday currency in the remoter parts of Argyll.

Action was called for and quickly. The guardian of the law and his unfortunate family were sent to Coventry. No milk, no eggs, no words. The police station was deserted, ignored, a virtual 'no-go' area. Within days his pleas for a return to Glasgow grew to an irresistible demand. His wish was granted, and a week or two later, the local 'bobby' returned to widespread acclamation. Common sense and the quiet word retrieved things and life returned to normal. I enjoyed other visits to Tiree before progress intervened. A time-and-motion study showed that it was more economic to fly officials in at 10am and out at 3pm the same day. Never again were we to be able to step beyond the image of the colonial administrator with briefcase and umbrella who came to speak and not to listen.

If that policy had not been introduced regional officials might have got to the bottom of the great attendance mystery on Coll. On the last Friday of the month it was claimed that hardly any pupils from outlying parts made it to the primary school. This conformed to no known patterns of truancy in the region, and many a head was scratched in Glasgow in perplexity. I was told years later that the parents were paid to take their children to school by car as there were no school buses. On the last Friday of the month, the Customs man was on Coll, a man with a passing interest in tax discs on windscreens. I don't know where the truth lay, but it's a far better story than is usually produced to explain statistical quirks. When last on Coll I was almost disappointed to see cars properly taxed — was it always so? Do they keep one or two 'legits' at the pier as a 'front'? Perhaps the coming of roll-on, roll-off ferries has widened motoring horizons.

As I began to become known in Argyll and, I hope, trusted, it was made known to me that every school liked to put on its best face to the director or other visiting dignitaries such as the dreaded HMI, easily detected close-up by their regulation issue black leather briefcase embossed with a gold crown. Their inordinate pride in these was a fatal give-away. It seemed at first sight reasonable not to inadvertently sneak up on a school. On the other hand a sow's ear of a school could be transformed into a silk purse given sufficient warning, and thereby inadequacies in teaching be disguised. There developed a good-humoured game in which the intelligence net of the schools did all in its power to 'spot' a visitor and spread the word in good time, and we, for our part, attempted to catch in the act (or non-act!) those few we suspected of a less than conscientious approach to their duties.

There is a story which, knowing the characters involved, is more likely to be true than not, of a group of HMI calling unexpectedly at Oban High School. After a few minutes with the head in his study, they were surprised, then flattered, to learn that the flag being raised on the pole at the front of the school was being unfurled in their honour. At last due recognition was being accorded to those appointed by the Queen in her wisdom to ensure high standards the length and breadth of the land. I subscribe totally to the alternative explanation, which was that the flag could be seen from several local primary schools, and that due warning was being given that the Sheriff had ridden into town.

I've never yet been able to work out if the teacher on the island of Kerrera could see it through her binoculars. Either way she had the extra advantage that her husband was the boatman and had several strategies for delay and warning. The first time I visited, my attempts to remain incognito lasted for about two minutes. 'How were the roads from Glasgow this morning?' was followed by 'From your hands I can tell that you are some kind of a civil servant.' One way or another, it was well into the lunch break, before we ultimately left the mainland, after he had begged my pardon and explained about adverse tides and the unreliability of his Seagull outboard motor. He needn't have bothered. It was a first-class school, and I knew it.

This was not the case with a school on the mainland, which was known to have the idlest, least competent head in the area. His survival for many years in his post had been purely down to a happy accident of geography. The school was situated close to the shore, but four miles up the only road, a dead-end. At the junction with the main road was a garage and petrol station, decrepit and seemingly deserted, like something from those Wild West adverts for spearmint chewing gum. The chance of the owner rousing himself to dispense petrol in those pre-self-service days was remote. But one thing galvanised him into action and that was the sight of a strange car turning up the road towards the school. He was on the telephone in a flash. Four miles of bumpy single-track gave the schoolmaster just time to tidy up, put on a suit, and produce spurious evidence of activity. It was not enough to fool the experienced eye, but sufficient to make you think that he might, with a good union rep, get away with it before a committee of councillors. He knew it and the oily charm of his welcome was more than enough to engender barely suppressed rage on my part, not least because I could remember the day when I almost had him — he'd been out of the school when the phone rang, and missed the first warning. Purely by chance I came face to face with his wife in her Morris Minor, radiator to radiator, bang in the middle of the longest stretch without a passing place. When she stalled the car and couldn't restart it, I knew that I had met my match — or had I?

The most doughty opponent can sometimes be taken from an unexpected direction — but how? I forgot about the problem as more pressing issues demanded my attention. A year or two later because of the need to give up July and August to budget preparations — the era of cuts/savings was looming — I resolved to take my annual leave in June, and to sail west from Kip marina in my Contessa 26, *Charisma*. Nothing like a stiff breeze and well-adjusted main and jib to dispel thoughts of work. I had, incidentally, rejected the suggestion that I equip the yacht with radio, 'in case they needed me'. The weather was idyllic, and we tacked through the crooked channel at Kyles of Bute, spent the night at my favourite mooring in Caladh Harbour, at the mouth of Loch Riddon, and next day rounded Ardlamont Point, accompanied only by a distant puffer and a nearby basking shark. Tiller in one hand, gin-and-tonic in the other, I ruminated on where next to drop the anchor. I fetched out the Clyde Cruising Club directions, flicked idly through the pages until by chance they fell open at a snug sandy bay, good holding ground, and sheltered from the prevailing wind. A building marked close to the shore looked to occupy a familiar site. I recognised it as the school and school-house. We arrived at dusk, dropped anchor, and spent a restful night. At 10am, next day I inflated the dinghy, rowed gently ashore and strolled up the beach. You can imagine the rest — the consternation, the chaos, the blustering, the excuses, the pleading. We settled on retirement at the end of the summer vacation, and I rowed back out, with a feeling of achievement — no more hapless youngsters, cross-eyed with boredom, far behind in their work. Years later when I met the schoolmaster in question again, he admitted that in retrospect, it was the best thing — a merciful delivery all round! To confirm that accountants have occasionally a sense of humour, I submitted an expenses claim to the regional treasurer, based on wear and tear on sails and spars per nautical mile, and received a note in reply regretting that only vehicles with hulls and sails painted in Strathclyde's ghastly colours were eligible for reimbursement.

CHAPTER SEVEN

Mulling It Over

MULL is one of my favourite haunts today. From Oban it is but a pleasant 45-minute cruise on the luxurious *Isle of Mull* ferry and from Craignure there is a wide choice of places to visit or linger in. Mull constantly surprises visitors because of its size; it has a land area not much less than that of Suffolk, which I was later to discover boasted several hundred primary schools. In Mull, if my memory serves me, there were only a dozen or so, mostly very small indeed. The region got off to a bad start with a suggestion from the policy planners that we could close most of them and build one 'in the middle'. Clearly these well-meaning chaps had not sampled the single-track roads of Mull, still less the middle which is rather bleak, high and understandably uninhabited. The suggestion was on a par with the one from British Railways London HQ in the 1950s which had suggested taking off the uneconomic winter boat from Fairlie to Millport on the isle of Cumbrae and Brodick on the isle of Arran and replacing it with a bus. Nonetheless there was one obvious candidate for closure: the school at Fionnphort, on the Ross of Mull, where the boat crosses to Iona. It was a damp, careworn Victorian dump of a place with a handful of pupils. There was a relatively modern school only a few miles of good road away at Bunessan, which could easily accommodate them.

Although I have grown doubtful about closing small schools just because they're small, there were really no strong arguments for saving this one. That did not deter the natives from opposing it tooth and nail, deeply suspicious of the region and its planners. I drew the short straw and was detailed to attend the public meeting to defend the closure. It was January. There was a gale and flurries of snow as the ferry docked at Craignure. I was accompanied by the district HMI, the much-loved Fergus MacDonald, and as we drove in his Wolseley 2200 through the snowflakes, we were in sombre mood. Our welcome was not overwhelmingly warm, and we shivered uncomfortably on the platform, as the good people of Fionnphort filed into the school with never a smile nor a wave. There seemed an awful lot of them to have produced six children. Plainly reinforcements had been called in from as far afield as Dervaig and Salen. Our arguments were brushed aside peremptorily and the humour which normally comes through in the Highlands was noticeably absent, although a couple of lads at the back who were passing around a half-bottle of Whyte & Mackay gradually grew more cheerful. Poor Fergus got the worst of it. Then it was the locals turn to speak, and they produced the best and most unexpected argument I have ever heard at countless of such meetings. The EEC, we were told, had plans, as yet unpublished, to revitalise the islands with a series of advance factories, the first of which (you've guessed it!) was to be in no other spot but Fionnphort. With hundreds of jobs in prospect we should be expanding the school, not closing it. Here we were, 40-odd miles from Craignure, itself a ferry trip from Oban, the first to hear this incredible — literally — news.

We escaped a lynching by a hair's breadth, and as we drove back to Craignure and our hotel, a deer leaped from a mound on our right, was silhouetted gloriously in the moon for a second before crashing onto the bonnet of Fergus's car. 'At least we are not going back empty-handed' said Fergus, tucking the poor animal tidily into the boot. By the time we got on the boat the next day, it had been butchered and parcelled into plastic bags, and the news had even reached St Andrews House. Fergus had to deliver a haunch of best venison to the chief inspector. Despite the 'news' from Brussels the school was closed, and although I go from time to time to Mull, I have seen not a hint of an advance bothy never mind a factory.

Fergus MacDonald was to become the closest of friends. Unlike many of his colleagues in those days, he was neither forbidding nor obsessed with his own importance. Uniquely, he was not a graduate, his days as a wartime bobby on the beat in Inverness having been followed by training as a 'commercial teacher' in the days before the image-makers transformed the subject into Business Studies. A tall gentle man in his late 50s, seldom seen with the black, crown-embossed case, he was revered by teachers and adored by pupils. I went with him once to another Mull school, I think in Calgary. As we approached it, he told me that he'd been there some years before, found the teacher ill, and had spent the day with the pupils. To what purpose I discovered on entering, when the youngsters squealed with joy, rushed into his arms and shouted to the teacher. 'Hey Miss, here's the nice man who taught us how to play poker!'

From Calgary we moved on to Dervaig, then if not now a unique village for Argyll — the only one I ever knew where in the rain the women wore green wellies and Burberrys, and which supported its own tiny theatre. It had been taken over by the 'white settlers' and the trouble was that they expected the school to be the same as the ones they'd left in Tunbridge Wells and Surbiton. We took pleasure in reminding them that Scotland still had its own legal, religious and education systems and that it wasnae going to change things in Dervaig just for a bunch of sassenachs! Perhaps it might be safe enough for me now to go back after 20 years. Just in case, I shall stick to Tobermory, one of my favourite haunts. The distillery-to-school ratio is not as favourable as it is in Islay but it's a lovely place.

I remember vividly sailing as foredeck hand on a yacht called *Faerie Nuff* on the annual Tobermory race in the early 1970s. We left Crinan at 4am, and reached the shelter of Tobermory all of 14 hours later, which time I had spent entirely on deck in howling winds and rain, as we beat interminably up the Sound of Mull, wind dead on the nose. The skipper worked on the 'exhortation by abuse' principle so it was as well that most of what he said was lost on the wind. Next morning, somewhat restored by a night in Bobby McLeod's Mishnish Hotel, I made my way unsteadily to the paper shop to purchase a *Glasgow Herald*, hoping to confirm that we had, as the skipper alleged, been first in our class. I clung to the counter, the ground still moving beneath my feet due to the waves and perhaps the whisky, and asked for my paper. 'Would it be today's or yesterday's you would be wanting?' the aged lady with the crumpled cardigan asked. 'Today's please,' I mumbled. 'Well in that case,' she responded, 'you'd be as well to come back tomorrow.' The logic was impeccable. It was probably her sister in the Post Office who advised a visitor to save money and send his postcards second-class. 'We do not have the facilities here to delay the second-class mail.'

On the road to Fionnphort and Iona from Craignure lies the hamlet of Pennyghael and on my way to deal with some trouble at the school on Iona, I chanced to stop at the school. In many ways I wished I hadn't. Despite an idyllic setting across the road from Loch Scridain, it was depressing beyond belief. Single-teacher schools are fine if the teacher is outstanding — it is quite common for pupils in them to see only a single face throughout seven years of primary schooling. If the teaching is uninspired, dull, or just plain inadequate, the effects hardly bear thinking about. This was such a place. There were no pictures on the wall, no pupils' work; dust lay on bundles of outdated text books. Eight desperate children sat imprisoned in a serried rank of old-fashioned desks, although new tables lay in plastic wrappings in the hall. In their eyes I saw mute despair. Teacher was huddled over a high desk such as I had found in my room at Whitehill in the 1950s, woebegone, lifeless. It was Dickensian without the beatings — there was no need, the urge to rebel was long gone.

In the course of the next hour or two, in as kindly a way as possible, I tried to suggest changes, improvements. I searched desperately for something good to say, but couldn't find a thing. The teacher was well-meaning, not knowingly idle, which made it all the worse. At 4pm the children having been mercifully released from their daily ordeal, we moved into the school house for a further discussion. The schoolmistress bustled about making tea, and produced a sultana-cake to accompany it. It was good; at least I could give genuine praise for that. 'Best I've ever tasted,' I heard myself say — understandable hyperbole. We parted on better terms but with the problems unresolved. A later visitor from the offices in Dunoon was so incensed that he took the old desks onto the beach and set fire to them, before unwrapping the new ones in an attempt to bring the classroom, symbolically at least, out of the 19th century.

The following autumn saw the occasion of the annual Argyll

Teachers' Conference in the Columba Hotel in Oban, where I was guest speaker. Isolated as the Argyll teachers are, this week of autumn half-term held under the pretext of in-service training, can and usually does become a thorough-going bacchanalian orgy, which only the fittest can survive. The official ceilidhs are followed by unofficial ones in the bar, which are then continued in the hotel corridors. I am led to believe that I went straight to breakfast from one of the latter and then delivered a stirring address an hour later. I am unable to confirm this from my direct recollections.

What I do recall is that the hotel lies on the pier where the delegates from Mull were to disembark. I went out to greet them. It was high tide and the gangway was steep and slippery in the rain. Down it staggered the teacher from Pennyghael, balancing precariously in her arms a huge cardboard box. When she finally reached the pier, she made straight for me. 'This is for you,' she said. In it was a huge sultana cake, beautifully iced, with a note thanking me for being so kind on my visit. I was very much moved by that tribute. The cake was very much moved when submitted to the tender mercies of my three young children. At the ceilidh the Pennyghael schoolmistress sang Gaelic songs in a clear sweet voice — if only we could apply our talents where they could be most useful.

When I had called at Pennyghael I had been on my way to Iona, where the grapevine had informed us that the recently-arrived lady teacher was 'acting awfy strange'. She had gone there from an inner city school to escape an unhappy past and to find peace. Her passion for cleanliness had at first gone down well with the mothers of her pupils — scrubbing of necks and behind ears was strongly encouraged. But when she turned her attention to the school playground, which consisted largely of grass, and complained to all and sundry about the sheep-droppings there, some unease crept in. This reached crisis proportions when she ruled that no sheep should be allowed anywhere near the school unless their continence could be guaranteed! With such a fixation it is hard to think of a less suitable place to take up residence than an Argyll island. I had barely time to exchange a sympathetic glance with the solitary boy who attended school every day with seven or eight girls, when the ultimatum was issued. It was a contest she could not win, and she didn't.

Last summer I could not help but notice that the manners of the sheep had regrettably failed to improve. I had crossed to Iona to pay a small personal tribute to John Smith, the former Labour Leader whom I had known at Glasgow University where we were students together. What might have been if he had not been struck down, like a predecessor Hugh Gaitskell, when all lay before him. A native of Argyll himself, he had more than once shown that he was aware of the work being done for education by the officers of the regional council. Now as cuts bite deep, much of the good work is being undone, much of the rich fabric destroyed. Where is the 'lad o' pairts' to come from if the quality of education in the Highlands and Islands is to come under threat yet again?

CHAPTER EIGHT

Islay Mist

TARBERT, or to be more specific Tarbert Secondary School, was and probably still is the epicentre of the schools' intelligence net. For the eye of the visitor Tarbert has many delights, from its harbour where fishing boats and yachts compete for berths, with the former usually winning, to its excellent fish and chip shop. For those in the know, the real activity is above the bustle of the main street. In the 1970s Neil McGill was headmaster, a charming bald-headed man, quiet in the manner of the Gael but with twinkling eyes which matched a wry sense of humour. Respected as he was by pupils and colleagues alike, the frequency of visitors from HQ had nothing to do with concern about the well-being of the school. To his skills as a delightful host, he added a unique ingredient: Neil was privy to supplies of malt whisky of a quality far surpassing what was available in the local licensed grocer. Its origins, coyly described as 'across the water' were concealed by its invariably being dispensed from a decanter. I was to learn that there was a subtle class distinction here, the 'lower classes' kept the same brew in lemonade bottles. In no circumstances was it to be found in a whisky bottle. It was said at that time that no Customs Officer stayed on Islay for a tour of duty exceeding six months. By that time he was reckoned to be 'turned' completely by the natives. It was during the latter stages of his decline, presumably, that the contents of decanters and lemonade bottles were spirited from

Laphroaig, Lagavulin and my favourite Ardbeg. Possibly it was explained away as 'the Angels' share'.

A visit to McGill's academy invariably followed the same pattern — polite discussions on the educational stories of the day, an enquiry after the health of his charming wife, Betty, a former HMI, and from Neil an invitation to the 'smallest of sensations'. At a time when alcohol was forbidden in Scottish schools, and I had only seen the odd bottle lurking in a filing cabinet in the occasional more liberalised Catholic school, this was a mark of trust and, of course, an invitation to join the conspiracy — one can imagine the headlines: 'Senior Regional Officer Found Drinking in Tarbert School'.

These concerns were easily dispelled and the divine malt, with a little water since it was clearly cask strength, was soon cosseting and relaxing the inner man. When tongues had loosened sufficiently in Neil's fine judgement, there came the ever so casual question, 'Will you being going down the Mull, or across the water from the East Loch?' The requisite information painlessly extracted, Neil would excuse himself, refreshing your glass as he left. Soon the wires were buzzing, alerting all the schools in the Mull of Kintyre and Gigha if that way you were bound, or to the command post at Bowmore, if Islay was the destination. Soon Neil would return, a pressing duty discharged, and his charm and wit would captivate the visitor further.

The invariable visit to Neil ensured satisfaction all round, and in collaboration with the Islay mafia on the ferry, ensured that however elaborate the feigned surprise, every school was on its toes to greet the visitor. There was one occasion only when the system let them down. Bound for Islay, my car broke down near Inveraray, a not infrequent occurence with an Austin Maxi — mine spent most of its guarantee year in garages dotted all over Strathclyde. I was rescued by the driver of a Ministry of Agriculture and Fisheries Land Rover, contacted by the AA, who whisked me straight on to the last boat. On arrival in Port Ellen I booked in at a B&B, whose kind proprietor lent me a car next morning, inadvertently contributing to my unintentional disguise. After a leisurely breakfast, I made my way along the straight road over the Laggan Moss to Bowmore, passing not a single car in the entire nine miles. Then it was on to a small school on the shores of Loch Indaal. It was a glorious morning; the larks were singing, and the oyster-catchers chattering on the sands. I found the pupils playing in the sun, and to my surprise the school door firmly locked. After chatting to the infants I made my way to the school-house, and knocked on the door. I heard a clock inside chiming ten. After a little while the door opened to reveal the schoolmaster, in his dressing-gown and slippers, munching a slice of toast and mar-malade. If not caught with his pants down, he certainly did not have them on. I envisaged a sequence of events similar to that when I had outflanked the school on the beach in the dinghy: an excuse at least. Not a bit of it. After but a moment's hesitation, he drew himself up to his full height, and said in a soft lilting accent, 'Mr Graham, if you had been kind enough to abide by the rules which we both know then neither you nor I would be facing this embarrassment.' I felt the ground shift beneath my feet, and a hanging offence being commuted before my very eyes. It took me all my time to avoid feeling guilty, if not downright ashamed!

The boot was on the other foot when overtures reached HQ from Bowmore that there was a desire for the secondary school to have a sixth form. In terms of educational viability it was a non-starter, but like Tiree and its aspirations to a four-year school, there were other arguments to do with keeping young folks on the island. In order not to raise hopes prematurely a small group of staff and parents asked for a meeting and that it should be confidential! That was a tall order. At their request I flew from Abbotsinch in the BEA Viscount, bypass-ing Neil McGill and the ferry. My arrival was not auspicious from the point of view of discretion. 'Good morning, Mr Graham, and welcome to the island' was the greeting from the chap with the 'table-tennis bats' who assisted the plane to its berth on the windswept tarmac. The taxi-driver told me how nice it would be if his Fiona did not have to go to the hostel in Oban as he drove me to the boarding-house which was in effect one half of the Royal Bank of Scotland.

There I was greeted effusively by the amply proportioned lady of the house, none other than the wife of the bank manager. As it was winter, I was the only guest. Dressed in a full-length diaphanous evening gown which gave her something of the appearance of a vast vampire bat, she fussed over me at dinner — cullen skink, salmon and cheese. As I supped my second cup of coffee she leant close to my ear and whispered, 'Drink up your coffee, or you will be late for your secret meeting!' It was therefore not entirely a surprise when I arrived at the hospitality room of the Bowmore Distillery — where else for such a meeting — to find an inner ring of the half-dozen or so I was contracted to meet, and an outer ring of another 30 to 40 ready to hang on every word. The outcome was fully covered in the local press, except for some reticence about the substantial inroads made into the hospitality stock.

On a pilgrimage to the distillery recently I was pleased to observe that Bowmore still carries on its own malting. There is nothing to match the sight of the barley lying on the stone floors, a foot deep, the heat rising as it germinates. As I watched the careful turning of the 'piece' with wooden rakes, as I had once done in the 1970s, memories of the whole episode flooded back to me but a return visit to the Bank House revealed that all had changed. The guide at the distillery remembered my hostess well and her eccentric dress; sadly she is no longer with us.

Changed too, no doubt, are the attitudes concerning propriety and behaviour. I remember a fairly wild party with some teachers at which it was boasted that of those intimately entwined 'not one was sitting on the knee of a legitimate spouse'. I recall that the martinet who succeeded Charles Edward Stewart when he moved on to higher things in Inverness was shocked to hear of a couple, both married, having an illicit affair and both on the staff of the same primary school. It is said that he pored over the Caledonian MacBrayne timetable for hours until he found the two schools in Argyll which were farthest apart, and posted one to each! It is not entirely certain that he applied this draconian solution universally. When himself enamoured of a young lady teacher she was soon transferred quite conveniently for Dunoon. I sometimes wonder what he would have done if he'd heard about the head of a school in Lorne, who, after a similar party, set off on the long winding road home, only to be overcome as he drove by an understandable lassitude. He was found next morning fast asleep in a lay-by by two policemen who, concerned for his health, drove his car home, carried him into the house and put him gently to bed where he was quite surprised to wake up some hours later. How many heads could be sure that their former pupils would treat them so benevolently if caught in such a pickle?

By now it will be clear why Argyll and the isles provided such a fascinating antidote to the daily burden of administrative life in Strathclyde, and although the memories are vivid, the visits grew all too infrequent. The Director of Education was seldom able to leave our fastness in Bothwell Street, and grew suspicious (perhaps rightly) of those who did. I subscribe to the view that one day out in the schools tells one more about reality than ten in the office. There is no more salutary reminder for the education chief of what life is really like than constant visits to the classroom and, indeed, the chance to teach children himself. Many a happy, sometimes difficult hour has been spent by me in large secondaries and small primaries. On one such occasion, I resolved to drop in on Strathlachlan School in Cowal, close to the caravan site on Loch Fyne where my family spent their holidays. The school was small and unkempt-looking, with a corrugated roof which had no doubt replaced the thatch. It was a hundred yards down a track from the tortuous lochside road and had but five pupils. I knocked at the door, which was opened by what I can only describe as an apparition. As she leant on the doorpost, ready for battle, her great arms crossed beneath her ample bosom, it was possible to detect the contents of recent meals down her front. A hand-rolled fag dangled from her lower lip and her hair had plainly not seen a comb in some time. I feared the worst, introduced myself and asked if I could take over the class for a couple of hours. To say that she agreed with alacrity would be an understatement. Donning a coat which might have come from Oxfam, and a hat which would not have sold at a jumble sale, she sped off leaving me to it. What a surprise lay in store. The pupils were lively, well-informed, competent and the hours sped by delightfully. Not for the first time or the last, from Ayrshire to Suffolk, was I to find that appearances can be deceptive.

Mark you, all in all I was relieved to find that a few months later Charles Edward had discovered a loophole in the school closure regulations which enabled a school to be closed 'temporarily' for six months and without a public inquiry if a structural defect was found. While this description might have suited the temporary schoolmistress, a more orthodox crack in the walls was soon diagnosed. The pupils departed for the excellent school at Strachur — one of many, by the way, where the head fired the boilers and cut the playground grass as part of her contractual duties. After six months nobody wanted to go back and the Strathlachlan teacher departed to live with her sister in Catacol.

One of the rich legacies bequeathed to Strathclyde by its constituent authorities lay in its residential schools and outdoor centres. Many of these were in Argyll, and they provided in the 1970s a much needed break for youngsters from urban life, whether they needed extra medical care, or simply had never been away from home and could do with a widening of their social and educational horizons. While Ardentinny remained closest to my heart, some of the others were equally memorable. Internationally recognised musicians and painters of the future gained valuable experience at the Art and Summer Schools at Castle Toward, from whose grounds exquisite views of sweet Rothesay Bay could be gained. During the school year, countless youngsters learned while there to appreciate and to respect the countryside. I like to think that the growing awareness of environmental issues springs from experiences like these. At Southpark near Ascog in Bute, girls from broken homes found respite and hope, and at Rhubodach overlooking the Kyles of Bute, handicapped youngsters were given an enriching experience, never to be forgotten. Outdoor centres at places like Blairvadach near Arrochar and further afield at Faskally in Pitlochry, introduced teenagers to sailing, climbing, canoeing, and orienteering which gave them lifelong interests and new horizons. This was achieved without recourse to the prevalent philosophy of teaching children by terrifying them. The challenge was gentle but persistent. It was invariably an uplifting experience to call in on one of these. Many of them are closed now or their future hangs by a thread. The need is as great as ever, but they are prime targets for the indiscriminate axe. Sadly, they can never be recreated. The vision which our forefathers displayed in acquiring them is not shared by the utilitarians of today — they have fallen victim to the belief that man lives by the three 'R's alone, and that there is no need to educate the soul, and liberate the inner person.

As my time in Strathclyde drew to a close, escapes from HQ became more difficult. Even business in Edinburgh could be disrupted by a summons to come back on the next train. I well remember setting off for Arran with a colleague, Iain Halliday, to consider some extension work at the secondary school at Lamlash, and call in at Corrie School, where the indomitable Miss Gracie had been in charge for countless years. We looked forward to three days on the island. As the *Glen Sannox* entered Brodick Bay, with snow on Goatfell, and the sun glinting on the castle, Iain said to me, 'What's the bet, there is a message to go back at the pier?' Sure enough there was a chap standing by the gangway with a placard proclaiming in large letters, 'Message for Mr Graham'. We passed him without a second glance, toasted the office's health at the Lagg Hotel, and phoned from the pier on the way back to check that all was well! Many worthwhile upgradings of schools resulted from our efforts.

Going is seeing and seeing is believing. The head of the school in Gigha complained volubly about the state of the pupils' loos — open-air earth closets, if my memory serves me. Architects sent to investigate reported that what with the site problems, difficulties getting contractors over and one thing and another, it would cost the equivalent of £30-40,000 in today's money to put in a couple of WCs. It was out of the question. That was small beer in comparison to the cost of recladding the face of Campbeltown Grammar School, which had been built to take on the full force of the Atlantic winds, with porous stone panels, but it was a lot for a loo.

We took a small posse of regional councillors across to the island. Gigha has its attractions from the views of Kintyre and Islay it affords to the glorious gardens planted by the Horlicks dynasty, but being caught short in a bleak schoolyard in February is not one of them. The councillors came, they saw, they shivered, and they authorised the work. Look ye and marvel when next you are in Gigha. I sometimes wonder if old Sandy, the taciturn tobacco-chewing seaman I worked with on the MV *Maid of Argyll* in the 1950s, had had his attitude to life soured by decent exposure in his native isle.

Just before I left Strathclyde news came of trouble afoot at a girls' hostel where the 12 to 18-year-old girls from the islands were boarded, most of whom only saw home during the school vacations. A stringer for a tabloid newspaper had heard that the ultra-respectable, strait-laced matron of this establishment might be having a quiet affair with the postman from Taynuilt. Indeed it was claimed that his bike had been seen at the foot of the fire escape long into the night. None of our business, we said. 'Guardian of all these girls,' the journalist replied. 'Think of the headlines. What an example to set.' We surmised that absolute proof was lacking, or the story would surely have broken on the front page straight away. It was decided to be on the safe side and send in our man in the area for a quiet word.

The matron was of demonstrably impeccable character, a pillar of society, an example to us all. As he approached the hostel, our man wondered just how to broach such a difficult, indeed delicate, subject. His unease did not diminish as she welcomed him, resplendent in her Sunday best, and ushered him into her private lounge. She served tea in exquisite bone-china cups, scones of her own baking, with napkins embroidered by her own fair hand. How on earth could he work round to the purpose of his visit? Buying time, he admired the flower arrangements, complimented her on her dress, beginning to verge on the incoherent as he strove to steer the conversation towards a tactful broaching of the reason for his visit. In his own words, he heard a voice which he only later recognised as his own, saying, 'I hear you are knocking it off with the postman from Taynuilt.' The matron leapt in the air, cups and scones and embroidered napkins flying everywhere, and burst into uncontrollable tears. Our man still wonders if he might have handled it another way. He took his leave, his warning delivered, if needed it was. I still wonder about the postman from Taynuilt. His bike was never sighted at the hostel thereafter. The tabloid remained opaque.

On leaving Strathclyde I missed Argyll and the isles a lot. I like to think that in return for the fun and the friendship so generously given, I helped in a small way to improve the quality of education, both for teachers and for pupils. Some of the corners that I and colleagues cut certainly led to improved teacher numbers and smaller classes, together with considerable progress in Special Education. Sadly, some of these were soon to be reversed by those less sympathetic to local needs. I was of course to find that there are just as many characters in Suffolk as there are in Argyll.

PART III

Suffolk

CHAPTER NINE

Sleepy Hollow

AFTER five years of Strathclyde, I felt prepared to tackle anything. What I did not want to tackle was a lifetime there. Wider horizons beckoned. Such were the promotion prospects in Scotland that, like to many a Scot before me, the high road south seemed the most attractive option. New appointments had been made to all the Scottish regions at the time of the local government reorganisation in 1974, and the incumbents were apparently in good health. Dead men's shoes might be a long time in filling. So I began to scan the vacancies columns in the English nationals. The first position to appear was that of County Education Officer, Suffolk. Where the hell was Suffolk? Above London and out to the north-east on the coast — it looked promising.

Soon the charms of that county became evident — very much 'out of the world and into Suffolk'. There was Constable Country, the Elizabethan splendours of Lavenham, the picture-postcard ford at Kersey (only later did I learn that the head there was an Esperanto nut!) and the sleeping, rolling hollows of High Suffolk. In contrast there was Ipswich, a thriving bustling town, and Felixstowe, a happy mixture of holiday resort and England's leading container port. Lowestoft to the north seemed cold, grim, and disaffected with rule from Ipswich, as did Bury St Edmunds, Dickensian and picturesque to the west. The scars of reorganisation were all too evident in Suffolk too.

Later I was to discover the coastline with the remoteness of Bawdsey, the beauty of Southwold and Aldeburgh (Benjamin Britten country) and the arresting bleakness of the marshlands. The highest point in Suffolk, just 276 feet (84.1m) above sea level, was scaled annually by the Beccles Mountain Rescue Team, who established base camps in the pubs en route, where they stored ropes and crampons. An acquaintance who was a geologist told me that apart from flint, there was no other natural stone in Suffolk and that folks would pay a fiver for an imported fist-sized rock for their gardens. Despite its undoubted charms, I thought of my beloved Argyll, and swithered.

Confident of instant rejection, I decided to apply and was to my surprise summoned for interview. There was a short list of six (there being no 'leets' in England). No two-minute interviews either. This was a two-day affair involving dinner with the leading county councillors and interviews with the Chief Executive, Clifford Smith, and other chief officers. The venue was Belstead House, a delightful residential centre near Ipswich, which had been in former times the Judges' Lodgings when on circuit, and latterly a teachers' training college for young ladies. Later I was to fight a back-to-the-wall battle to save it from councillors embarked on a cost-cutting spree. It is still there.

It was all so civilised compared to Strathclyde. Power lay in the hands of the dominant Tory group, but they were for the most part old-style Tories, farmers and landowners, and titles abounded. The Education Committee was chaired by Richard Harwood, a genial and caring man. His full committee met but four times a year. There was freedom of action for officers within an atmosphere of trust, as long as not a penny more was spent than was absolutely necessary. Suffolk prided itself on its low spending — there were no councillors' junketings, the chairman of the council drove his own car, and county hall was a converted prison, the only claim to fame of which was that in 1936 Wallis Simpson had gained her divorce in the adjoining court prior to marrying the abdicated Edward. There was no civic pride, but no glass-palace extravagance either.

The dinner was a splendid affair, the interviews thorough and the risks of appointing an officer from an alien system, manifest. The risk was taken, and when, after an interminable wait in the anteroom with the other aspirants, I was invited to go back in, no one was more surprised than I. After the formalities, I enjoyed a toast given by Kenneth Kemp-Turner, the Chairman of the Council, which he followed with a question. Would his opposite number in Strathclyde Region tolerate an Englishman in the job? I told him I doubted it; the English are a more tolerant race than the Scots. With a significance which escaped me at the time, this was the very day that Margaret Thatcher became Prime Minister. Although it was May, as a kind of portent, snow fell and lay by the trackside as my train home rattled through Colchester and the enormity of it began to sink in.

Apart from the need for the family to start a new life and make new friends, there was the recurrence of the 'Sleepy Hollow' syndrome. Why bury oneself in rural remoteness in a minor authority? Why abandon all the work on the national stage which Strathclyde had brought? Why risk all in an alien culture where no one had heard of me, and where I knew so little that when I took my first delegation of councillors to Elizabeth House, home of the DES (Department of Education and Science), I got them lost in London's traffic. I realised that there was no point in taking cold feet. The die was cast and from the day I arrived in Suffolk, the challenge proved totally absorbing. With a population of 600,000 it was the 'right' size for an education authority. Unlike Strathclyde, a chief could know his secondary heads well, although he could spend a lifetime visiting primary schools of which there were more than 500, many of them small and rural. People were friendly and laid back and when I first met the unions, I came within an ace of getting it disastrously wrong. This was no place for confrontation, no Red Clydeside. Quiet co-operation was the style. Likewise there were no religious undertones. Protestant, Catholic, Buddhist — it mattered not a whit. In eight years I never found out anything about the religious affiliations of my staff, nor of course did I want to.

It was refreshing to find that unlike Strathclyde then, and many other places now, officers were expected to get on with administering the service, maximising resources, and having professional advice accepted at face value. Hugh Fairlie of Renfrewshire would have relished the atmosphere. To be fair, the top Tories were more paternalist than dedicated to education, but their hearts were in the right place, as long as all the bricks could be made without straw. They saw me as a kind of exalted farm bailiff — left to get on with it, provided the budget balanced, and the harvest of 'A' levels was gathered in. Only twice did I ever see them really outraged at county council meetings. Once was when the Labour group proposed the rating of agricultural premises, and the other when the embryo Liberal group proposed the banning of straw-burning! Later, Tory ranks were swelled by the estate agents and small shopkeepers, and things changed for the worse. But that was still some years away.

Problems abounded in the education service and in the Education Department, whose address I was able to have as 'St Andrew's House' when it was renamed upon upgrading. The irony may have escaped the chief executive. The first problem was that the deputy education officer had resigned. An old Etonian, laid back to the horizontal, and a man of exquisite culture, he did not even wait to meet a barbarian Glaswegian, but took himself off to run a group of girls' schools in the home counties. This was probably a wise move all round — even his resignation letter ran to 12 pages — but it did leave me with a problem. All the other senior officers were aspirants to the now vacant post, and I could hardly reveal to them the parlous state of my knowledge of the English system. It was bad enough to meet deputations of school governors — a new experience for me, because then there were barely school boards in existence in Scotland — but what were the subtleties of 'aided' and 'voluntary-aided' schools? I never really did find out. In time I learned that 'caretaker' meant 'janitor', and that 'exercise book' meant 'jotter', but I gave much innocent amusement to the schools of Suffolk.

I also met the redoubtable Anne Broderick. As Secretary to the former Chief Education Officer for many years, she had become better known than he was, and on the whole the schools preferred to deal with her. I never quite cured heads of asking to speak to her, when perchance I answered the phone. I won — just — a battle of wills about my preference for dictating letters which due to the ropiness of her shorthand resulted in her fertile imagination often bringing back to me letters infinitely better than when first dictated. Her revenge was to employ her 'Miss Jean Brodie' accent (acquired during a spell in Edinburgh) whenever she took a call from north of the Border.

Her former boss proved more of a problem. John Hill, a compulsive worker, had retired at the age of 64 due to ill-health, but was in no mood to leave his empire to my tender care. Somehow he had managed to retain a place on every committee from university courts to governing bodies, and on these the county of Suffolk spoke with two voices, usually discordant. I grew used to lectures on how it should be done, taken in good part, as he had been a distinguished man who had risen from humble beginnings to an exalted position. But there came the day when we stood in line to be presented to Prince Michael, the Duke of Kent, (Hill resplendent in his CBE) and he introduced me as: 'My successor, much in my shadow, and with so much to learn.' Over his head I received a delightful glance from the Duke, quizzical and amused. When Hill decided to lead the public protest against the first school closure (why did it have to be in his village?), I decided that the time had come for action. I arranged a meeting with him and produced a note in his handwriting dated two years before, proposing the very same closure. I then surmised as to what the press would make of it all, which effectively accelerated his withdrawal to real retirement, devoting his energies to his work with national charities. I made a mental note to go gracefully myself when the time came, and never to interfere with the work of a successor. I think I managed both.

I found that two of my fellow chief officers seemed to regard the ratepayers' money as their own, and were as tight-fisted as the councillors. One remained so until his retirement. The county treasurer was an ersatz Scot — kilt and country dancing but with a southern accent and a certain vagueness about the whereabouts of Auchenshuggle. Every penny (or bawbee) spent was for him a penny wasted. Although willing to overlook the cost of his own son in a class of one in Northgate sixth form, he regarded education as a necessary and restricted evil, and looked forward to 'cuts' with undisguised relish. Our jousts were epic, memorable even. His greatest triumph was to winkle out the 100 teachers too many which we had in our schools. Mine was that he was so pleased he did not look for the other 300! What unconfined joy there was when his smile, likened to the burnished brass plate on a coffin, was replaced by that of Philip Atkinson whose philosophy was that money was there to solve problems, not create them, and to enrich, not deprive. I gave his predecessor a bottle of Ballantine's when he left and I'm told he checked through my expenses to see if I'd charged the county for it!

The other one who inclined to the parsimonious was the chief executive. A man of great talent and diplomacy, initially given to leaving all his pens on his desk at night 'so as not to use the ink for private purposes' and to travelling second-class even when it meant standing all the way to London, he came to see the folly of cuts beyond reason; to trust that schools spent wisely and carefully, and to take on environment ministers Michael Heseltine and Nicholas Ridley in the time of greatest trauma with Margaret Thatcher. Children in Suffolk owe him a great deal: in return his much merited CBE was delayed for years through petty spite. The last time I saw him in London he was distributing three packets of sandwiches from the Liverpool Street Station buffet among six hungry councillors who seemed to find his careful husbanding of resources a mite on the frugal side!

I'll never forget the day I was summoned before these two for inquisition. It transpired that a school cleaner had worked for the second week of the school holidays rather than the first, by arrangement with her head. When pay for the work which was indisputably done was claimed, the treasurer had refused on the grounds that it was for the wrong week. A widow with small children — too bad! My staff had then waited until the first opportunity to claim it for her under a different heading and been found out. The Star Chamber wished to ascertain whether I was implicated. I was not, but I offered them my hands for the manacles! There was a deathly hush. The lady got her money, bureaucracy lost out. Another lesson learnt — stand by your staff if they are right, even if the methodology is questionable!

The starkest contrast with Scotland which was immediately apparent lay in the attitudes to the value of education. In Scotland, there is a consensus that it matters above almost all else, a gateway to advancement, a treasure in itself. In the South, this is not so. It is a privilege purchased by the middle-classes, not a birthright of all. In Suffolk there was a feeling that a certain amount of it was a good thing — useful so that workers could do what was required of them, but not something which should lead to too much independence of thought or expansiveness of expectation. Suffolk education committee held in my time an impromptu debate on the merits of reducing the school leaving age to 12, of which more anon. Middle-class demands for standards were singularly lacking, partly because Suffolk had to an extent missed out on the Industrial Revolution and the middle-class to go with it, partly because they tended to buy education as a commodity. When the cuts came, there were few voices to be heard in protest, in contrast to the vocal, well-argued protests from the parents of Newton Mearns and Milngavie whom I had met in Strathclyde. Expectations were low in Suffolk and standards were modest. Sixteen-year-olds in Debenham or Eye were aghast at the prospect of travelling ten miles to join a sixth form; some had never been to Ipswich or Norwich, never mind London.

Under the lax supervision of my predecessor, schools had largely gone their own way. As a result some few were superb — at least a match for the best in Strathclyde, and probably more creative and imaginative. At the other extreme were some so poor that in despair I at times contemplated a fast train north of the Border as the best way out. Misguided, bewildered, certainly not evil in intent, there were schools which Scotland's informal national curriculum would not have permitted. Seeds were early sown in my mind of what was required in England — no wonder government ministers described the system as 'patchy' at best.

There was much to do which required new staff, new ideas, new challenges and the removal of some who were well past their sell-by date. To be fair, many of them knew it and were happy to accept the prospect of early retirement — an everyday occurrence now, a novel procedure in the late 1970s. Of the 50 or so who went then, I value letters from not a few, written thereafter, of gratitude and appreciation — they have lived long and happily. One of them, a retired secondary head, has proved magnificent as the organiser and controller of all the sailing activities of the county. He alone shared my horror at the lack of training, rescue, and safety facilities in Suffolk. We haunted boat sales for second-hand dories, outboard motors, and life-jackets. When I recalled the safety standards I had known at Ardentinny, I despaired.

A revolution, it was no less, began to take place in Suffolk, and 'Sleepy Hollow' came to life. In 1983 the *Times Educational*

Supplement sent a reporter to investigate the changes. His article entitled 'Sleepy Hollow Awakes' begins:

'Wednesday afternoon in Bury St Edmunds, a pleasant and prosperous market town in the west of Suffolk. The sun beats down as the pens of pigs and cattle are despatched at bewildering speed to their new owners — slow-moving men who seem little impressed by the auctioneer's chatter or his attempts to demonstrate the quality of his goods by bringing them to life with a whack on the rump. I try to avoid blinking as six piglets go for £28.'

He goes on to contrast the image with what he found — a 'Suffolk Curriculum' worked out by teachers in co-operation with parents, and industrialists beginning to abandon their prejudices about standards and basics, willing even to join in to provide relevance and resources. I was described as 'an ebullient Scot' who had quit the tenements of Strathclyde to find in Suffolk a potentially high-quality teaching force with the dedication to work well beyond their contracted hours. There was a contrast with the dispirited and union-minded souls in industrial areas where the final bell was the signal for a 'Le Mans' exit from the school car park. The article goes on to list the achievements from 'Suffolk Science' adopted by 40 other authorities and selling in the Far East, to the Suffolk Farm Project, and pioneering experiments in schools/industry partnerships. I learned things from the article which I did not know were happening — conclusive proof that if you pick and enthuse the right people they will soon leave you far behind.

To my intense satisfaction, many of my colleagues in Suffolk were to find themselves in great demand as their fame spread. Soon subject advisers such as our scientists Leslie Smith and Mike Coles, and Maths guru Peter Reynolds, were roaming the land as was Sylvia Richardson, a curriculum planner par excellence. I remember with particular affection our historian, David Penrose who, each year was to be seen on sunny summer days dressed up as Cardinal Wolsey, being conveyed to Christchurch Mansion by horse and cart (we too could not 'afford a carriage'). On arrival he would climb down with difficulty but dignity to receive homage from primary pupils in period costume who had spent the morning acting the parts of Tudor servants and grooms. David would make his way to the dining-room where a groaning table bore all the trappings of an Elizabethan banquet prepared by the infant scullions below-stairs. He did the spread justice while the youngsters ate their packed lunches outside — some customs never change!

As a result of Suffolk's growing reputation, I was soon to find myself once again on a national stage, and a very different one from that of COSLA and St Andrew's House (the Edinburgh one, that is).

CHAPTER TEN

Characters and Closures

AS a new chief, I decided to get to know heads and teachers in the
county. This meant the discipline of setting aside at least one day a
week on safari. In 1979, before the full force of the attack on local government, it was possible to abandon the paperwork and the politics
and think about the provision of real education, and where better to
do it than in the schools? Almost every visit revealed some new gem,
often to do with 'the office', where what seemed reasonable and sensible could look very different from the chalk-face. All too often
bureaucrats, individually doing the right thing by the book, collectively can turn a policy into a bunch of bananas.

Although visits from the chief were a novel idea, greeted at first as
'spying', the warmth of the welcome became one of my abiding memories of Suffolk. It gave an opportunity for praise to those in education, and elsewhere, whose efforts all too often go unnoticed — the
good, average, faithful servant. On my return to HQ, I always put my
gratitude and praise in writing. Later I was to find these letters
(known as 'AGTs' — or A Good Thing) framed and displayed proudly.
Suffolk was an idyllic place for visiting schools: very few inner-city
areas, lots of rural splendour, and always a hostelry for an al fresco
refreshment in the summer, on the edge of the village green.

I decided to meet all the primary heads in the four areas of Suffolk,
and started off with 150 or so in county hall. I delivered what I

considered to be a spell-binding and inspirational address and, after the dutiful applause, asked if there were any questions. Up rose a figure near the back of the hall who would have looked shabby even at a meeting of new-age travellers at Stonehenge. After a pregnant pause he said, 'Why have you brought me all the way from Bawdsey to listen to this rubbish?' My response was feeble, my curiosity was aroused. Next day, having summoned him to my midst, he appeared dressed inprobably as a morris dancer, bells jangling tintinnabulously, thudded an army haversack with a protruding pig's bladder on the top of my desk and said, 'This is now two days away from my pupils; your reason had better be a good one!'

I never did find out about the costume, but I did learn that he was Head of Bawdsey Primary School. I nicknamed him Bawdsey Bill.

Bawdsey Primary School became first priority for a visit, and I made my way through Woodbridge and Melton, past the villages on the shores of the River Deben to one of the remotest spots in England. It was at Bawdsey Manor that Pitt-Watson had carried out the research on radar which had saved us by allowing vectoring of Spitfires in the Battle of Britain. The school was less grand than the manor — red-brick, surrounded by grass and what appeared to be either an Anglo-Saxon settlement after a spot of rape and pillage, or a grossly neglected allotment. It was Bawdsey Bill's practical garden for his dozen or so pupils. The schoolhouse was surrounded by piles of wood, broken machinery, and rusting tractors — this was the 'adventure playground'.

The classroom was chaotic, Bill perched on a high stool like a time-expired garden gnome seemed to be presiding over a rehearsal for a riot. Time for decisive action — a display of awesome power on my part. But I had come armed with a disconcerting fact: the best prepared and liveliest pupils who entered Farlingaye High School each year came from Bawdsey. Furthermore there was a unique 'feel' about that room which I have never experienced before or since. It lived, it throbbed, it pulsated with excitement; it was magic by any standard. 'And those who came to mock, remained to pray.' I became a convert.

As time passed I felt I was beginning to win. When I next held a meeting of primary heads, Bawdsey Bill came in an approximation of a suit, and when a newly-appointed head tackled me rather brusquely,

Bill leapt upon him with the words, 'How dare you address our chief in that impolite manner!'

Bawdsey Bill achieved a national reputation by proxy when years later I was involved in setting up a national scheme for appraising the performance of teachers. Unions and civil servants were obsessed with the need for rigid criteria, and checklists of good and bad practice. I could well imagine what any school inspector or teacher training college would make of Bawdsey Bill with such a system. And so the instructions to the working party were to find a scheme which would recognise the obscure genius of a Bawdsey Bill, as well as the more conventional skills of teaching. The scheme now in place largely achieves that and there are teachers all over England who ought to offer him a silent prayer of gratitude.

None of this impressed Bawdsey Bill. Still less was he impressed by the news that his school was to be proposed for closure. He led the predicted parental revolt with vigour but without rancour. There was by this time a Mrs Bill, a fighter of all causes green and anti-nuclear and a follower of the Greenham Common school of fashion. Unknown to me a tiny Bill had been gifted unto them. Came the night of the public meeting in Woodbridge, the hall was packed and hostile, the local press poised for blood, the chairman of the primary subcommittee visibly unnerved, and myself poised to explain how closing the school was going to be good for them — a blessing in disguise!

As I rose to speak I was aware that the Bawdsey Bills were sat in the front row, but a yard in front of me, and that there were three of them. As my peroration began, Mrs Bill wrenched open her ethnic blouse, and clasped baby Bill to her left nipple where it began to suck with noisy enthusiasm. The odds, never in my favour, began to tilt. I faltered then rallied. At this point the infant was unclasped from the left nipple, the right breast exposed, and baby Bill transferred his attentions there. It was too much. The education committee in their wisdom later decided to leave well alone. I've known schools saved by a whisker, but only once by a nipple! When I left Suffolk, the oddest but the most genuine letter of regret bore a Bawdsey postmark.

Bawdsey was not the only school that faced closure. Of the 300-plus primary schools in Suffolk, perhaps 100 could count the numbers of pupils on two hands or at most three. Unlike those in Argyll which

I knew so well, many of these were within a mile or two of the next one. In some cases you could see one village from the next. Where one of these was a damp decaying Victorian slum, and the other modern with space to spare, there was only one logical answer, educationally and economically. In my experience when numbers fall below 15, the 'group dynamic' — the process by which children stimulate each other and learn from each other — is lost. Even with the best of teaching, it is hard to achieve a breadth of experience. The rub too is that it is hard to attract the best of teachers to such small schools. Seven formative years with a poor, dull teacher does not bear thinking about. I can never escape a mental picture of the teacher at Pennyghael in Mull, and the mute appeal in the eyes of the eight youngsters slumped at their desks. The educational reasons for closures were sound. So too were the financial ones — far better to concentrate scarce resources on buildings, heat and lighting, and books where they were most needed.

Parents and villagers in Suffolk had different ideas, although sometimes the more discerning parents felt trapped by the arguments about 'saving the village' voiced by worthies whose families were long past school age. To them it was the rural depopulation argument which was uppermost. First the pub, then the shop and now the school. Statistical evidence to the contrary — that villages often thrived when parents felt free to send their youngster elsewhere — met with blank disbelief. It felt 'right' to see the children walking to school and hear their chatter as they crossed the village green. Teachers who wished to stay convinced parents that tiny classes and individual attention outweighed all else. With no absolutes in terms of proof, and closure seen as the work of remote unfeeling bureaucrats at county hall, the scene was set for confrontation. National societies sprouted up to brief villagers on procedure and obstruction. Gone were the days when a director of education could advise his committee to close a few schools at the end of term. For good or ill we were now at the other extreme — a year's consultation, political battles in committee, and a final decision taken by ministers on the advice of civil servants in Whitehall and after pressure from local MPs who were 'nimbys' to a man — school closures were essential to remove surplus places but not in their back yards.

The most blatant of these was the indestructible John Gummer, MP for Suffolk Coastal, and perpetual cabinet survivor. While demanding cuts in Suffolk, he defended the continued existence of the smallest secondary school in the county. The evening before the final decision, he had dinner with Sir Keith Joseph, the then Secretary of State for Education. To my great relief he failed to convince Sir Keith, and the closure was confirmed. Ever the man to be on the winning side, John Gummer phoned me the next day. His words I shall never forget. 'Hello, Duncan, I am using my new car phone to let you be the first to know that I persuaded Sir Keith to close the school for you!' Now there's a consummate politician for you — never be seen on the losing side.

To the credit of the education committee we pressed ahead with the closures of the worst and smallest schools. Drinkstone near Bury St Edmunds is one I shall never forget. Damp, decaying, with galloping rot, it was not the place to be on a winter's day — particularly if you were a pupil and caught short. It was a 50-yard sprint to the earth-closets, without roof or plumbing.

At the public meeting, the attack was led by a formidable lady with the plummiest of accents. Her bosom heaved as she spoke with passion of 'her' school. When asked how many of her own children had passed through the doors of the school, she replied in a voice of booming horror, 'Good God, not mine — jolly convenient for the servant's nippers.' She then spoke passionately in defence of earth-closets and their hygienic qualities. When I dared to suggest that she must therefore have them at home in the Manor, she threatened to have me sacked for impertinence to my betters. We did close Drinkstone — eventually. When I visited it last autumn, the playground had become so overgrown with brambles that we were able to make a blackberry pie and jam as well. Of the earth-closets nothing was to be seen, but the undergrowth looked particularly lush where they had once been.

We were less fortunate with Somerleyton near Lowestoft. Although internally a slum, it rejoiced in a thatched roof, and in summer honeysuckle grew round the door. When I took a civil servant to see it, the flowers surrounded a lovely, smiling, matronly teacher, with a cherubic curly-haired five-year-old in her arms! Only a barbarian, surely, could destroy such a scene.

As if that were not enough, news came through the network of the aristocracy that Lord and Lady Somerleyton were not best pleased. Hardly time to look them up in Debrett's when I was summoned to an audience with the local MP who was none other than Jim Prior, at that time Secretary of State for Northern Ireland. His farm south of Lowestoft had become fortress Prior, with three rings of defence, and even as we sat in his study, the shadow of an armed guard passed across the patio every 30 seconds. The price to be paid for great office can be high indeed. A man of charm and integrity, he accepted fully the arguments for closure, advised me to carry on, but to expect the worst for the county and, sadly, the pupils. He seemed to hint at royal influence. As I passed through the defences between the farm and rural Suffolk, I reflected on the gulf between real needs and political decision which has widened still further since then.

Next day, a Saturday, as I lay half-asleep watching the news I noticed on TV the president of the United States' helicopter touch down on the lawns of Windsor Castle. As the Queen stepped forward to greet him, the hushed voice of a lesser Dimbleby was heard to say, 'and at her Majesty's side is her aide-de-camp Lord Somerleyton.' I knew then in my heart that Somerleyton School would not close. We had it re-thatched instead — it looked even nicer, but no warmer or drier.

All in all, about 40 schools were closed before the Government's policy of allowing schools threatened with closure to opt out of local authority control, demoralised councillors in Suffolk as elsewhere. Whether it was worth the effort is now to me an open question, although the misuse of resources is obvious. In many cases, after the trauma of closure, the benefits of attending a slightly bigger school, still tiny by city standards, often became clear, and parents were happy with the outcome. No villages to my knowledge 'died' as a result. Two things I remember vividly still: firstly, the unadulterated horror of many villagers at the prospect of sharing with 'them' up the road. Xenophobia begins at home. The other is how unprincipled the 'white settlers' who move in can be when in opposition to a proposal. The nastiest closure, involving personal threats and abuse, was in a lush suburb of Ipswich and the worst physical abuse and violence I was to witness was over the bus dispute in Capel St Mary, just south of Ipswich. But that in itself deserves a chapter along with the story of Sudbury Upper School, run in the Tory heartlands by a red-hot soviet.

Consultation and Confrontation

CAPEL St Mary, a village whose original houses had been submerged in rampant suburban developments, has left on my heart scars like the 'Calais' that Queen Mary claimed would be found on hers. It was a flashpoint for a confrontation over 'bus passes', the education officer's nightmare, and the middle-class demand for involvement in decision-taking — one of the often illusory privileges of Thatcherism.

The law was clear — a yard over three miles from school (two for primary pupils) and free transport to school was an entitlement. A yard under and it was not. There were no sub-clauses dealing with divided villages or streets, no concession for dangerous roads, just the measuring wheel of the surveyor. Early in my career I learned that openly bending these rules, however nonsensical the situation, was fatal. If five yards over the magic limit was permitted, why not ten, then 20? It was too slippery a slope to slither down. That is not to say that an innocent mis-measurement could not be the same as a blind eye. I well remember condoning that ploy when we found in a Catholic school in Greenock that the boys' gate was just under two miles from a large housing scheme and the girls' just over.

In Capel St Mary the distance was comfortably under three miles from the secondary school at East Bergholt. On foot, however, pupils had to cross the A12 dual carriageway, one of the busiest roads in south-east England. Pupils from Capel St Mary had been allowed to fill vacant seats in school buses passing through the village for some years. In 1982, not only had their numbers grown above the capacity of spare seats, but Suffolk was also forced into draconian cuts which meant that not even the lucky ones who had enjoyed the concession could be accommodated. To have given way would have raised riots in a dozen other areas of the county. A compromise was offered: buses at cost price, at a modest £17 a term. In other areas parents were willingly paying £30 a term. It was rejected outright by enraged parents. The county council invited the parents to take them to court, if they felt it was acting illegally, but they declined.

After three deadlines had been postponed, the great day dawned. The parents had found a 'village Hampden' in Derek Hurley who spoke eloquently about 'fascist officers' and 'callous councillors'. The national TV networks were there to see a storming of the £17 buses for which no passes had been purchased, followed by a crocodile of pupils wending its way along the verges of the A12. That night a sit-in was staged at the school by about 50 pupils, whose parents left them there without bedding or food. What then emerged was that some had been authorised and coached to be rude and disruptive beyond belief. The head and colleagues went far beyond the call of duty, as did my own welfare officers, to care for them. We drew the line at feeding them, and were roundly abused for our pains. Thereafter, before being taken to school in the Volvos and the Jags, egged on by their parents, children physically assaulted drivers and laid traps to push bus officers into girls who then accused them of sexual assault. I witnessed one case where a boy knelt behind a member of my staff while another pushed him so that he fell over the first boy and damaged his back. He was then accused of attacking the boy and knocking him to the ground. All this was accompanied by the foulest language I have ever heard, inner-city Glasgow not excluded!

In douce Suffolk this was unbelievable. From educated, affluent parents it was inexcusable. They lost public support after a week or two of purgatory for my staff, and reverted to the Mercedes and the Rover, but what damage had they done to their children? They lost many hours of schooling, and presumably learned that physical assaults and deceit are legitimate in pursuit of one's ends. Their parents called their children 'pawns', but who had made them so? More fundamentally, it was the first occasion on which it became clear, if only in retrospect, that consultation does not guarantee parental success, and that cuts can hurt. The fact was that authorities like Suffolk did not have the 'fat' to absorb the 'economies' so beloved of government ministers in the last decade.

At that time I was involved in a brush with the prime minister who had demanded that Suffolk save £5m by trimming its top-heavy bureaucracy. My response, that their total cost, including myself, was £2m, leaving £3m to come from fewer teachers and books, was not well received! Local government was becoming a convenient scapegoat. Its vital role as a counterbalance to central government in a country without a written constitution was to be so undermined as to leave it as an impotent pensioner of Whitehall. Capel St Mary was a watershed. The incompatibility of consultation and parental involvement on the one hand, and lack of resources on the other, had been graphically illustrated.

This was not the only problem with school buses in a county where two-thirds of pupils needed transport of one kind or another. Suffolk hit the headlines again when an aspiring Liberal politician and the parents in a village near Bury St Edmunds convinced *That's Life* that a grave injustice had been perpetrated by bungling bureaucrats. With the film in the can, and Esther Rantzen poised for action, I was contacted as an afterthought for a comment. I shall never forget the panic on the face of her 'young man' when he learned that they had been completely misled by the parents. The programme went on as if I had never spoken, fatally flawed on every count — a travesty of the reality. I have not once since watched *That's Life*. In the future, I was frequently to face interviewers whose line had been so fixed beforehand that facts made no difference to the outcome.

Capel St Mary was not the only surprise which Suffolk threw up in 1982. Rumours had reached me that all was not well at Sudbury Upper School, a 13-18 school in the south-west of the county, and that the school was in effect being run by a small group of staff who were bypassing the head. By coincidence I attended the school play and while most of such visits were duty, with agonising imprints on the posterior from hard seats, this one was different. I think it was *Pygmalion* but it may have been another of the works of George Bernard Shaw. In a quiet respectable market town, this was an electric performance — naughty words, strong sexual nuances, and remarks about the head which were actionable. It was a close-run decision to see it through without intervening. In effect the gauntlet had been deliberately thrown down in an effort to 'break' the head. His predecessor, it emerged, had spent his final years quietly in his room, legitimising the actions of a soviet of five staff including a deputy head and the immediate past-president of the National Union of Teachers in Suffolk. The new head had taken them head-on. A cricketer in the Botham style in his leisure hours, he approached them with flailing bat, and was no match for their guile. While the chairman of governors and some others were worried, a minority of the staff appeared to back the rebels.

An enquiry was called for. After interviewing all 60 members of staff, a remarkable picture emerged. Many said that they had been intimidated, some claimed physically, by the soviet. The big five seemingly made up the timetable and could 'reward' their followers with 'nice' classes and Friday afternoon off. They hired, fired and promoted staff. They had hand-picked the prefects to ensure control of pupil affairs. They controlled the school office — in short they were in complete control. The head had refused to co-operate, so he would have to go. Their politics were linked to local Labour circles which would cause trouble if a Tory council took them on. Absolute concrete proof of their activities was hard to come by — that is the nature of things.

What to do? A quiet word with NUT officials proved that they were worried too but did not relish taking on their past-president. Meanwhile the school was a seething hive of fear and discontent, with staff leaving without replacement, and pupils' work suffering. Such was the skill of the soviet that few parents were complaining. Could this be happening in 'Sleepy Hollow' Suffolk? Nothing even in Strathclyde came near this. Officers and members of the council were tempted to look the other way — but not for long. Nettles had to be grasped.

It was recognised that, unfair though it was, the head would have to go. He had lost too much face. So must the ruling five. The governors would have to accept this, risk the consequences and restore the school to normality. To their eternal credit union officers came to the same view and confined themselves to finding the best terms for all six. My neck was on the line, not least when, accepting my advice, the governors stated publicly that it was their respect for me that had swung the balance!

In the end the rebels all went quietly. Two of the wiliest heads in Suffolk were drafted in one after the other to quell the minor players and within a year Sudbury Upper was a good 'normal' school again. Instead of party political posters, the hall once more contained adverts for debates, sports and the tuck shop. The lessons to be learned were many; among them that decisive action, while better late than never, is not as good as early nipping of trouble in the bud. I later learned that Sudbury had in the 19th century been a radical hotbed — seemingly old habits die hard.

On a more cheerful note, the experience of the play brings back memories of countless nights spent at school concerts and plays, in spite of the seats, rewarding and often surprising as the levels of ambition and achievements rose over the years. You will understand if I say that I never again wish to attend another *Oliver* or watch people 'Fiddling on the Roofs'! One annual fixture that I never missed was the Christmas nativity play at an infant school in Ipswich. The head, who wore a 'cloche' hat so constantly that I began to think she slept in it, invariably created hopelessly ambitious twists to the traditional plot. Inevitably the proceedings unravelled at the seams, and her temper rose to match, until the muffled curses and thumps behind the scenes spilled forth onto the stage. In the best year she came to blows with a mother understandably incensed after Miss X had kicked her five-year-old on the shins, audibly questioning the authenticity of his parentage. They don't make them like that any more. She had to go. The hat was firmly in place as we bade her a fond farewell.

When things became stressful, what invariably worked for me was to visit a school for handicapped children. How better to restore a sense of proportion than a day with inspiring youngsters and dedicated teachers overcoming great obstacles, rejoicing in every step forward, however miniscule. Out of many, my favourite was Belstead

School in Ipswich. Hilary Birkin and her colleagues believed fervently that self-respect comes from self-sufficiency. Every step to independence — holding a spoon, or a cup, tying a shoelace, could mean more than five 'A' levels did to a gifted child. Years later it gave me great satisfaction when Kenneth Baker accepted my advice that the national curriculum should be for all children of all abilities. What a pity his successors saw fit to include the Belsteads of this world in their league tables, inevitably at the bottom: 'O grades ... nil.' How could they so crudely measure the true value of human achievement?

CHAPTER TWELVE

Politicians — Local and National

WHILE relationships with minority parties in Suffolk were important, it was the dominant Tory group that mattered in the early 1980s. I still cannot quite believe that today a Labour administration with Liberal support presides. No wonder the Tory-controlled counties in England had shrunk to one in the mid-1990s. In the end the abuse and neglect of local services, and of their own staunch supporters, has had its just reward. Loyalty to the cause was unquestioned in the early Thatcher years, and the drip, drip of poison effective. It was directed largely at that delicate relationship between officers and members which characterises local government at its best. In theory members make policy, officers carry it out. In practice it requires trust and flexibility on both sides. The government view was that officers were suspect — devoted to undermining the crusade, and unduly protective of services because of their professional loyalties.

Of course there could be some little truth in this, but overall it destroyed trust, led to the devaluing of professional advice, and caused great strain particularly between those elected members furthest from services such as Education, Highways and Social Services, and their chief officers. Those who made the 'mistake' of finding out too much rapidly lost their cutting zeal, which created party tensions as well. I remember one such 'cutter' despatched to 'get' education for £5m. We sat him down with the budget, gave him a red pen, and left him for a day. Periodically I was called in to explain the consequences of a chop here or there. By 5pm he had earmarked a possible £10,000 saving in Theatre in Education (live performances for schools)! In time he became a staunch ally. A little knowledge is a dangerous thing; safer not to have one's views sullied by the facts.

Behind the cut and thrust, there remained in Suffolk genuine respect, and a civilised, at times elegant, approach. The chairmen (and woman) of the education committee deserve a chapter to themselves. Equally fascinating were the power brokers — chairmen of policy committees and the council. I did not envy them — caught between the treasurer, party instructions from Smith Square, and a county education officer who advised his committee of the need to increase spending, and to balance quality against 'economies'! Some of them demonstrated that the 'characters' in local government were far from extinct. More polished than Tom Stanton or Davie Miller, usually Eton and the Guards, they could carry by their presence a clout which sometimes the cloth-capped councillors of Port Glasgow could not muster. Mind you, they were no sharper or more cunning.

One was Mary MacRae, a spinster lady of manly frame and booming voice, beside whom Margaret Rutherford would have looked an inoffensive midget. When angry she started speaking before she reached the door of my room — I could hear her warming up as she approached! With Eilean Donan Castle (the ubiquitous one in the *Scottish Field* calendars) in her family, half of Loch Fyneside near Otter Ferry, and sundry estates elsewhere to add to those in Suffolk, she was not short of a million quid or two. If there was the wrong end of a stick to grasp, she grasped it. The places where angels feared to tread were her constant haunts. She was, in short, un-briefable. This had refreshing results as witness when she greeted an EEC deputation in Lowestoft with the puzzling words, 'Who knows, if you behave yourselves, Britain may one day join the common market.' Life was never dull.

One fateful day she lunched not wisely but too well at the Angel in Bury St Edmunds with the local MP, at that time Eldon Griffiths. Over coffee and brandy, the conclusion was reached that the school-leaving age should best be reduced from 16 to 12. Too much education was making the farm-workers discontented with their lot, and those who toiled in the chairman's Suffolk vineyards were getting above themselves, confused by a surfeit of liberal studies. To convince Sir Keith, they needed a persuasive paper — that fellow Graham would oblige.

After a confused call (that is, even more than usual) my card was marked. I consulted the permanent secretary at the DES — a man who as occasion required could top anything 'Sir Humphrey' ever said. His advice was to produce a paper so opaque that it was meaningless, so wide anyone could subscribe to it, so far from requiring action that Sir Keith could endorse it without either hurting feelings or tabling legislation to reverse the course of education in the 20th century. It was a tall order, but I suppose that of all the papers I ever wrote, many of national significance, this was probably the finest. Everyone was delighted. I was treated to dinner at the Angel by Eldon, and had a letter of thanks from Sir Keith to frame!

I once had the experience of visiting the chairman at her home — a surprisingly modern house built like a Roman villa, with splendid apartments to house family treasures, contrasting with exquisite embroidery which her mother, then in her 80s, had made. Tea was served on a silver salver, with extremely beautiful bone china and resplendent antique teapot. Incongruously sitting beside them was a common-or-garden milk bottle! Although her hospitality was beyond reproach, it was widely noticed that when she gave a county council reception, the wine tasted like the dregs from the barrels in the vineyards, which allegedly it was. This made good economic sense, I suppose, but was not calculated to make you rush out for a bottle of Chateau MacRae.

I had and have a lasting affection for her. In her way she had a devotion to public service which was greatly to her credit. So too did Captain Robin Sheepshank (without the final 's' and touchy if one got it wrong!). Although perplexed and surprised by the crudity of some of the government ministers he met — who could ever forget a cursing from an irate Nicholas Ridley, apparently smoking three cigarettes at once? — he gamely tried to meet party requirements and at the same time do what he could for the council. His wife was unforgettable — straight from a Brontë novel. Beautiful and exquisitely frail, she walked with a stick, martyr to an unspecified ailment. It was noted that it grew worse when gentlemen were in attendance — I have seen a veritable squadron of admirals vie to assist her up the steps into the Ministry of Defence. When alone Lady Sheepshank could walk unaided. I was clay in her elegant hands, ensnared hopelessly by that smile, those eyes. Ah well! Many of us have nurtured aspirations above our station.

Like many of his class in Suffolk, behind Robin's fairly modest title lay impeccable connections. On one occasion when Prince Charles visited the county, he requested an informal lunch between engagements. In the end only Robin, myself and Prince Charles foregathered for the finger buffet. When the Prince enquired after each of the chairman's numerous offspring in turn and by name, I was impressed! Although my three were doing well at School in Felixstowe, they did not figure in the conversation. Still, it was my first opportunity for an informal chat with a royal, and it remains a highlight. I was impressed with the prince's genuine compassion and understanding of problems faced by under-privileged youngsters. After Captain Sheepshank and Mary MacRae, we began to move into new and less interesting Tory Council leaders.

As Suffolk emerged from 'Sleepy Hollow' and its reputation in education circles grew, we began to receive ministerial visits. News came that Sir Keith Joseph was to spend a day with us: this was an opportunity not to be missed to show him both our successes and our resource problems. Where would we take him? Lowestoft was always neglected and had a superb special school. There was the Northgate question. A pattern for the day emerged. I met him at Ipswich Station and we headed north — we had even hired a car, hang the expense! He was a delightful man, willing, even eager, to argue a point, but hopelessly imprisoned in monetarism — throwing money at problems didn't solve them he claimed. I take the view that it sometimes helps, especially when the lack of it *is* the problem. Sir Keith got off to the worst possible start at the station. When asked by a reporter about Suffolk's cash crisis, he had replied, 'What crisis?' It was soon a banner headline in the *Evening Star*. He was superb with the children in the special school, sitting cross-legged on the floor, his staff banished to another room. He overstayed his time and left visibly moved.

Back to Ipswich we sped. Northgate High School was the biggest secondary school in the town in the worst buildings in the land. There had once been two schools — boys and girls, each with a frontage nearly 400-yards long, with virtually nothing behind. It reminded me of those facades they put up for Wild West towns in Hollywood — all image, no substance. By the early 1980s the place was in terminal decay, and boasted no less than 27 wooden huts behind the facade. As Sir Keith had vouchsafed in the car the view that buildings did not matter ('You should have seen my public school'), we had work to do. In the end it was the Suffolk winter that prevailed. Carefully placed in the full force of the wind for an extended chat with the head, the secretary of state wilted before our eyes. The government rule was no new schools where there were existing 'roofs over heads' however decrepit. Could we help him to bend them? We certainly could! Yes, it could be a good exercise for his own DES architects. Yes, we could finance by selling land; mercifully that was the one thing Northgate had plenty of! Could we undertake the project in stages? Yes, we could. The deal was informally struck and stuck to. Northgate High School is now one of the finest school buildings in England. When the final stage was opened recently (I was not invited) I wonder how many of those present knew to what and to whom they owe it all.

In the gathering gloom, amidst driving snow, we made our way back to the station. It was like a scene from *Dr Zhivago*, Sir Keith topped off with his fur hat. As the train drew in, he embraced me with tears in his eyes: 'Thank you, I go back a sadder and a wiser man.' The train pulled slowly into the night. It changed nothing; the budget was still slashed.

A few months later, his successor appeared in Suffolk, Mr Kenneth Baker no less. Little did he or I know then how our paths would cross in the era of the national curriculum. From the start he seemed disinterested, rushing through a primary school in less than ten minutes with hardly a word, leaving speechless the head whose reward for 50 years of loyal service was to meet the great man. He came to life only when TV cameras appeared, when he kissed the nearest available child! He snubbed the leading councillors by refusing lunch in order to speak to Tory agents whom he'd invited into our Belstead House, and ducked out of his last appointment to rush off to antique book shops, his great passion at the time. I was not impressed and could only compare him adversely with his predecessor. In effect he did himself, as I was to learn, less than justice that day. I suppose I was lucky not to be in Suffolk when Kenneth Clarke or John Patten visited, if they ever did.

CHAPTER THIRTEEN

Chairmen and Woman

AS has been mentioned before in connection with Renfrewshire and Strathclyde, the relationship between senior officers and the chairman of their committees is crucial to success or failure, and as to whether day-to-day life is congenial or hell. It was during my time in Suffolk that nationally relationships began to change for the worse. As in so many areas of our life the new Toryism seemed to set out wilfully to destroy the subtleties upon which our nation's good government has been founded. To what extent the effects were accidental by-products and to what extent by design, is for debate. Certainly the potent memos to council leaders from Smith Square were designed to destroy mutual trust, and to diminish confidence in professional advice. There is to an extent a case for this; professionals can be too close to their subject, Masonic rituals can be practised, and self-indulgent complacency can creep in. But a good chairman should be well able to counter that without coaching from central office. Unchecked, one outcome was a complete breakdown of trust, with the 90's ministers seeming to reject as 'conspiracy' every piece of advice they chose to find uncongenial.

In 1979 in Suffolk, the balance was as yet undisturbed. The conflict between councillors, whether forced or willing to make cuts, and officers seeking to defend services was gradually to change that, as was the shift in Tory personnel from landowner to estate agent. Richard

Harwood, Chairman of the Education Committee, represented the best of paternalism — denigrated by Labour, but as good a motivation as any when allied to a calling to public service which had existed in the Harwood family for generations.

Youthful and puckish in a manner belying his 50-odd years, Harwood was a man of immense charm and ability, receptive to change where it was required, and, unlike some of his political colleagues, anxious to improve the quality of education in Suffolk and to increase the staying-on rate beyond the age of 16. At that time Suffolk had fewer sixth-formers pro-rata than any other county in England, an eloquent tribute to educational apathy and low expectations. When he and I took part in a phone-in for parents on Radio Orwell, we got no calls at all and had to invent questions for each other to survive for 60 minutes (excluding the adverts). On Radio Clyde, such a programme could jam the switchboards an hour before the programme was due to go out!

Richard Harwood lived with his extensive family at Bentley Hall — a minor stately home which rejoiced in a perfectly restored mediaeval hall, financed by grants from preservation bodies which had succumbed to the Harwood charms. He had recently sold off his prize Jersey cattle herd in response to one of those cyclical slumps in the market provoked by the inexplicable workings of the European Agricultural Policy. Forty years of breeding bovine perfection had gone, and now, like so many Suffolk farmers, Richard was an arable farmer, which meant bouts of activity, sowing, spraying and harvesting, but mostly boredom. He had the time and the energy to devote to education. We made a good team.

The first task was to find the scope for 'cuts'. That word was never used in public — euphemisms such as 'savings' or 'improved efficiency' were employed. Cuts became an annual ritual and a painful one in Suffolk where spending on public services had been traditionally parsimonious — or 'prudent' if you were that way inclined. There was little 'fat' to cut. How I longed for Strathclyde which now seemed positively profligate by comparison.

So we turned to 'making best use of existing resources'. We looked first to school meals, where the cost had led to a decline in uptake, and therefore an increase in subsidy to no less than £4.6m. We agreed

that abandoning meals was not an option for us (in deeper Tory terri-
tory like Dorset, it was). We believed that there were social and nutri-
tional benefits which mattered. No factory or workplace with several
hundred present each day would do without its 'heart'. As the
Siberian winds of a Suffolk winter blew across the plains, the
prospect of five-year-olds without hot food was not easy for us to contemplate.

The service was revolutionized, placed on a commercial basis
which is now commonplace, and which saved both the service and
money. I never dreamed as a young assistant director in the 1960s
that 20 years later I would be conversant with the variable cost of an
individual chip in Lowestoft or Bury St Edmunds, or the relative merits of hot plates and bains-marie. I still treasure a picture in the *East
Anglian Daily Times* of the chairman and myself tucking publicly into
'Suffolkburgers'. Looking at it now, I am irresistibly reminded of the
ineffable John Gummer stuffing a similar product into the mouth of
his first-born to prove that we had nothing to fear from BSE.

In spite of the pitfalls, Harwood next decided on school closures. To
give the thing a positive feel, and because he had a genuine vision, he
decided that the way forward was not random closure of Victorian
slums, but a return to first principles. If we were to start afresh,
where would we build schools and of what size? We would compare
this with the existing set up and then … ! His 'greenfield' policy was
doomed from the start. He was not the first, nor will he be the last,
politician to learn that being right is no defence. He failed to carry or
consult his party bosses. Councillors everywhere can support cuts
enthusiastically until their own school is threatened. If only one at a
time is up for closure, a chairman can generally get enough support
to carry through his policy. If he threatens them all at once, his fate
is sealed. Alas, poor Richard. Could I have given him better advice? I
felt guilty, but I did warn him.

Richard's loss was Felicity's gain. In the frantic rush to fill the gap
after Harwood's resignation (to spend more time with his family, ironically enough!) it was felt that a true-blue Tory was required, and one
who could be leaned on by the party leaders; no fancy stuff, just savings painlessly achieved. They seemed at first sight to have chosen
well. Felicity Cowley, a vicar's wife from Aldringham near Leiston had

a style of her own, but was patently in awe of her masters. She was the epitome of the Tory lady. In retrospect she seems to have been perpetually dressed for a garden party — picture hats, floral dresses draped about her ample bosom. She gushed bonhomie and goodwill to all men (particularly men!). Visits to the vicarage were sheer joy. Charles, her husband, was larger than life too.

He had lost a hand in a previous existence, and with its artificial replacement he could pour a mean gin. I confess now to have more than once reeled down the drive after 'open house' which by custom followed Sunday morning service. Invitations to these were much prized — amongst those we found ourselves rubbing shoulders with, were Princess Margaret, Sir Peter Pears, and the headmaster of Harrow, in whose chapel Charles frequently preached. He was without doubt the finest deliverer of a sermon I have been privileged to hear. His were short and pithy. They were so funny that laughter echoed through the aisles: then with exquisite timing Charles turned humour into a message so telling as to be profoundly unforgettable. He may have caused his bishop a few anxious moments, but in return he was an effective ambassador for Christ — accessible, convincing not in spite of, but because of, his foibles.

Felicity was at her best with her family, amongst whom the most amusing was a daughter living in London who was a raving leftie, prominent in crusading for 'dubious' causes and a rampant feminist to boot. She insisted in addressing her mother as 'chairperson' — anathema in Suffolk and still to me — such a graceless abuse of our language. It was about then that the person sent in during a Ladies' Test Match to hold the fort was described as a 'Night-watch batsperson'. Enough said.

I became (professionally) fond of Felicity. She was in all honesty not ideally equipped for the pressures of office; she cared, which ensured that soon she would be unable to reconcile her conscience with cuts in the classroom, but was apparently incapable of rebellion. She took abuse personally, and there was plenty of that from the teachers' unions and the press. I felt it was my job to protect her as far as I could, without giving up my stout defence of teachers and pupils, but it was not easy.

We staggered from crisis to crisis. A visit to the Radio Orwell studio for a phone-in is etched in my memory. The Labour spokesman was there, and the subject was school transport — shades of Capel St Mary. If not red-hot, the lines were at least lukewarm. The first caller asked his question and the presenter turned to Felicity. Her mouth opened but no sound emerged. He tried again — a strangled gasp emerged — no more. She had 'frozen'. To this day whenever I stand up to speak, I am haunted by this memory. Could it happen to me? We got through the programme thanks to the kindnesses of the Labour chap who refused to 'shop' her, and by dint of my fielding answers by commencing with: 'The chairman believes that ... '

Worse was to follow. There was a teachers' strike over pay — a feature of the early 1980s when teachers, although hard done to, seemed obsessed with losing goodwill by refusing to supervise school meals and bus queues. She agreed to a public debate with three union leaders, briefed by myself, and accompanied by Sir Eldon Griffiths, MP. I looked forward to a safe seat in the stalls, not least because my underlying sympathies lay with the teachers.

The hall filled to overflowing, the natives were decidedly restive, the banners draped from the balcony were uniformly hostile (and, having been created by teachers, misspelled). An ominous undercurrent was palpable in its intensity. I shrunk into my seat. The local Tory agent appeared, to announce that Sir Eldon had been 'unavoidably detained' but sent his best wishes. Felicity visibly paled, and then she shook. She rose to her feet; even at ten rows back I could see her swaying, the hat accentuating the gyrations. The chairman opened her mouth — once, twice, three times; not a sound emerged! We had been here before, but not facing up to a lynch mob. Then she spoke. 'My county education officer will now explain why my party has had to impose some minor adjustments which will entail the sacrifice of only a few hundred jobs.' She had handed me the ultimate poisoned chalice. Seemingly exhausted, but clearly relieved, she sat down heavily, and closed her eyes. I can remember every millisecond of every second, of every minute of the next hour and a half. My credibility with both sides depended on neutrality, not appearing as an apparatchik of the Tory or any other party. Suffice to say that at the end of the evening Felicity revived sufficiently to propose a vote of thanks, and it was seconded gallantly by the president of the National Union of Teachers.

It was decided in the inner sanctums of the party that Felicity had to be 'stiffened' — 'bolstering' was not an appropriate word here. So Richard Hickson was drafted in to push the party line, and, I suspect, to sort me out too. A pig-farmer, I had come across him before. The agricultural college had applied for a new pig unit more in keeping with modern practice than the ancient one they had. The six pig-farmers on the county council pounced — this was going to be good sport. They demanded a joint technical report from myself and the county architect and looked forward to eating us alive! Suffice it to say that the deputy architect and myself absorbed ourselves night and day for a month in pig husbandry, and wifery. A unit was designed, the plans submitted, and the inquisition began. There is nothing like brassneck and a bit of jargon. Not only did we survive, but the unit later won an award. There were two rewards. One was that the college, the fount of all knowledge porcine, moved pigs illegally a week after the unit opened, and the chief constable (the swine) deliberately chose to have me charged with the offence! Not many chief education officers have been admonished for illegally moving pigs within three weeks of their arrival. Perhaps it is this distinction which has resulted in one of my close friends in Cumbria being a pig-farmer, one Mike Smith. A national leader in his field, Mike has certainly not made that mistake. The other upshot was that Richard Hickson came to education with a score to settle.

The inevitable happened. Closeness to the action is a great teacher. Richard was soon as determined as Felicity to protect 'his' service. The chairman of the policy committee darkly accused me of deliberately 'turning' them and forcing them to go 'native'. While I am happy to plead guilty, in reality it is much harder to savage a public service when you can see only too clearly the consequences and can see beyond the stereotypes. Teachers in Suffolk were not profligate peddlers of new trendy methods, but hard-working, orthodox and caring. Later I was to see the same phenomenon when John McGregor was Secretary of State for Education, put in to sort out those liberals who had 'gotten us into this fine mess'. Within a year he had to go — he was listening and wavering. The exception to the rule was to be his successor, but more of that later.

When Richard Hickson and Felicity Cowley began actively to

oppose reductions in the budget, all hell broke loose within the Tory group. It was not a pleasant time either for them or for myself. Whatever they did to save money legitimately was opposed on the NIMBY principle by their colleagues. When they balked at damaging cuts, they were castigated. My own loyalties were cruelly tested. When the invitation came to a National Education Conference in Newcastle, we fled North for a few days' relief.

Newcastle was an ironic choice of venue. Monuments to T Dan Smith were everywhere, testimonies to municipal grandeur and in Felicity's eyes hopelessly profligate expenditure of public money. She strove to prove her political virility by a series of controversial interventions into the debates — no freezing here.

By the time of the banquet she had made quite a name for herself. It was a sumptuous affair, which in itself offended her greatly. As a gesture she refrained from eating, restricting herself to liquid refreshment. Entertainment followed — clog-dancing and a spirited rendition by a folk group of Blaydon Races in which Felicity joined with a will. Then a band appeared, the red carpets were rolled back and the dancing commenced.

Felicity chose to dance. She decreed an arbitrary ladies' choice and selected me. It was nominally a quick-step. At no point in the proceedings were we together in terms of beat, but in other ways we were intimately attached. If Felicity was a 'stately English galleon' I was deeply enmeshed in the rigging. If you recall those Hollywood movies with the nightclub scene, when all the other couples stop to give space and appreciation to, say, Ginger Rogers and Fred Astaire then you have the picture. The band maliciously prolonged their spirited rendition of *I Only Have Eyes for You*. When they finally relented we returned to our table to tumultuous applause. Felicity fortified herself and I must confess I did too. I reckoned too soon that the ordeal was over. Out of the corner of my eye I saw a fellow chief education officer whispering to the bandleader who turned to the microphone to announce the next dance. 'Ladies and gentlemen, I understand that the chief from Suffolk is a Scot. He will, I am sure, be delighted to lead off with his charming chairman in the next dance ... THE GAY GORDONS!'

It was the last fling — literally. On our return, and to their eternal credit, Felicity and Richard opposed at County Council cuts in the next year's education budget. It was a hopeless, courageous, unavailing gesture. The heroes were forced to resign the next day. Fêted by the public, ostracized by their fellows, their political careers were effectively over. My admiration for them and my affection for Felicity is undiminished. The pupils of Suffolk owe them much. Felicity was thereafter offered insultingly minor offices, which she declined with dignity. There will not be her likes again. Charles, though retired, still preaches with a will in pulpits around which sit the 'great and the good'.

I was getting through chairmen at an alarming rate, and the quality of education in Suffolk was improving in spite of the pressures — some might say because of them. What —or rather who — were they going to try next? The answer was Sir MacDonald Miller of Glenlee, Bart. He had been Jim Prior's election agent in Lowestoft for years, was widely experienced, and would 'get a grip' on education. I feared the worst — not least because the title was so odd, and he clearly did not hail from north of the Border. Bets were taken. Graham would be cut down to size this time. In vain did I protest that it was not me, but reality, which had struck down the others.

We met in an atmosphere of gloom and suspicion. Donald was palpably apprehensive that I would 'get' him or 'turn' him — infect him like some dreaded virus. Tea was served, with those ghastly little plastic containers of milk. After a minute's fumbling, the new chairman squirted milk over his suit, shirt, tie, and, as we later found, his socks. From that moment on, it was my first duty to open these wretched containers for him wherever we went. It's hard to be a stuffed-shirt in these circumstances. I refrained from any kind of pressure, and let him learn for himself and he did. A more subtle politician than Felicity, he played a longer game, was deaf to many appeals from the service, sadly unable to appreciate the value of things like the youth services and adult classes — which he dismissed as 'Painting and Macramé' — but he was a robust defender of schools and the three 'R's. He lectured central office on the folly of their ways, and the limitations of market forces, citing the Suffolk Schools Orchestra and Choir which could never be self-supporting but which launched many a musical career.

The annual Easter concert at Snape was a jewel in the school year. The Maltings provide a concert hall which is attractively spartan, and perfect for acoustics. We attended many concerts there given by artists of international standing, but the Suffolk schools event was the highlight. To stand at the interval on the steps of the bar, cocktail in hand, watching the sun set over the remote but beautiful marshes, blending the call of the curlew with the echoes of the music was bliss! A month after the policy committee decided that music tuition was suitable for 'downsizing' Donald invited its members to a party at his expense after the concert. I can recall a perfect 'Easter Hymn' from *Cavaleria rusticana* and songs from Britten's *Noye's Flood*, and a blockbuster Mozart finale. They reprieved music at the full council meeting next afternoon!

In spite of the grandeur of his title, MacDonald lived modestly in a small Tudor house, just north of Halesworth. A tall angular man in his 60s, with twinkling eyes, a shy smile, and a shining pate, he had little of the vanity which tends to afflict local dignitaries. However, he did cause consternation at a school opening in Pakefield. His speech was typical — it was councillors who built schools, never architects or builders, still less education officers. Then he stepped forward to unveil the plaque. As he pulled the curtains aside, his eagle eye spotted at once that his 'Mac' had become a 'Mc'! His wrath was unconfined and all too obvious. Never was there a quicker scurrying to rework a brass plate — hang the expense in this case. Years later when the National Curriculum Council (NCC) offices were due to be opened by the secretary of state and the stone had just been engraved with the name of John McGregor, he was replaced by Kenneth Clarke. The stonemasons of York, God bless them, carved a new one in a day and a half!

Later Donald apologized — he was intensely proud of a name which had been disgraced by his father, who had lost the family estate in south-west Scotland and dissipated the family fortunes in equal measure on wine and women. Donald had striven manfully and successfully to restore the good name if not the fortunes.

It was during Donald's period in office that things were calmest for me, giving time to do what I really wanted to do: to visit schools, reduce bureaucracy, and seek to raise standards and aspirations.

There was time to enjoy some of the social life of an English shire-county at its best. Events ranged from set-pieces like the Suffolk Show, (where amongst the stands, those showing the work of schools became a feature, and a pleasant surprise for those who thought that craftsmanship had disappeared) to garden parties; some set against the backdrop of stately homes, with marquees, brass bands and champagne, other smaller intimate ones drifting into the soft Suffolk evenings, where one could imagine one was sitting on a veranda in the long-lost colonies, a living part of a Somerset Maugham novel. I appreciated then how pleasant and unassuming the true nobility can be. My wife and I lunched alone with the Duke and Duchess of Grafton in a summer-house in the grounds at Euston, their estate near Bury St Edmunds. The duchess served the meal (no doubt laid out by her staff beforehand) and regaled us with discreet tales of her experiences as lady-in-waiting to the Queen. As I was soon to find out in Humberside with royal visits, the attempts of social climbers to ambush the royals provide quite a challenge for their staff, requiring everything from tact to unobtrusive man-handling. It was at this time that 'walkabouts' were in vogue, and the duchess had had to organize a 'conveyor belt' system to deal with the bouquets and presents given to the Queen.

Shooting was great sport in Suffolk, and although no expert with the gun, (to an extent that skill has been acquired in Cumbria more recently under the stern tutelage of the redoubtable Norman Dunn, gamekeeper at the Winderwath Estate), I used to enjoy the spectacle of the titled nobs resplendent in their tweeds and caps. It is an odd convention which places them in the hands of the gamekeeper, so much their inferior in social rank but who controls the shoot like a leader in the field of battle. The keeper is a general marshalling his beaters, his flagmen (whose white flags — often a stick and a plastic sack — encourage pheasants to fly high), the 'dogmen' who retrieve the game, and finally the pheasants, whose co-operation cannot be guaranteed.

Two events stick in my mind. I shall never forget watching as a portly gentleman, plus-fours lowered to half-mast, leaned against an oak tree while an eminent Harley Street surgeon prised pellets from his ample posterior with a penknife. He had been bagged by a bishop!

Some time later I overheard a belted earl ask a local physician to check over his butler who had not been too well — indeed he did look rather on the seedy side. 'Have you checked your cellar?' was the response. The earl dismissed this unorthodox diagnosis as far-fetched. 'James is not the type.' Two days later he phoned the doctor, 'My God, you were right!' The tribulations that beset the rich.

My own sporting endeavours were confined more modestly to the golf course. I played regularly at Felixstowe, reputedly the oldest sea-side course in England, which boasts two Martello towers and, in winter, winds which come straight from Siberia. These can cause hypothermia in anyone unwary enough not to be fortified with a hip-flask. Incredibly, each year on Burns' Day in January an intrepid Scottish team, sporting their kilts to a man, took on the 'Auld Enemy'. They may have wondered where the wind was coming from but they certainly knew where it was going — not least the one who, congratulated on the pristine freshness of his balls, confided that his wife cleaned them with Duraglit.

Each year the club played a match at St Clements, the only mental institution in Suffolk with a golf course in its grounds. The inmates seldom excelled at golf, but one of them obsessively raked the bunkers in the nude — a practice yet to find favour at the Open Championship, notwithstanding the streaker who appeared on the 18th at Royal Lytham and St Annes this year!

At this time I found myself drawn increasingly into work on the national scene in England. I had expected to leave that sort of experience forever when I left Scotland, but I became an adviser to the Association of County Councils, as I had been to COSLA in Scotland. This in turn led to my appointment to the Burnham Committee, that great English institution which settled teachers' salaries. Its structure was Byzantine. There were no less than 80 protagonists on each side, employers and unions. There was an independent chairman, and a senior civil servant representing the secretary of state, who carried an ill-defined form of veto, to be deployed whenever a settlement beyond government guidelines was in prospect. It was largely charade — a heavy disguise for imposed settlements. As I have already mentioned, because of its sheer size, it was difficult to find venues even in London, and very often it was the seedy ballrooms of decaying

Victorian hotels which became the backdrop to the slow-motion action. You can imagine how long posturing can take, with council politicians divided by party, and half a dozen rival union leaders with images to preserve. Many of the meetings were all-night affairs with hour upon hour to while away while the leaders met 'behind the chair' — usually a room with too many creature comforts to encourage brisk decision-taking. What a contrast with Scotland, where Keir Bloomer for the teachers' side, and myself for the management were sent off by the full body of 16 to work it out and report back within the hour.

The English scene is much bigger and less intimate, inevitably, than the Scottish. North of the Border, the same folks tend to appear on curriculum, examination, and negotiating bodies and, until 1995 at least, all the directors of education could get round one table. This led to an ease of communication, a commonality of viewpoints, and an ability to compromise lacking in England. It could of course lead to an incestuous, closed, magic circle. In my experience it is a risk worth taking. South of the Border, a multitude of examination boards, 120 LEAs (Local Education Authority), six unions, and a mass of civil servants who do not even know each other is a recipe for confusion and procrastination. In spite of that, I enjoyed the English scene — the vistas, challenges and scale more than compensated for the frustrations.

From 1985 the Burnham Committee was engaged in an attempt to define for the first time what the duties of a teacher actually are. Opinions varied as to whether this was the end of professionalism ('teacher knows best') or an overdue attempt to bring in discipline and value for money. The jury is still out on whether the gains have exceeded the losses. Doctors and nurses have been through the same hoop. In most respects it was a two-year waste of time. With ill-timed arrogance Kenneth Baker threw out an agreed settlement, the product of sweat, tears and realism, and imposed his own. It would have been even worse if the civil servant who spoke for him had not diplomatically chosen to go to the loo for an extended period, thereby missing the chance to exercise his veto. Even Baker could not get him for answering the call of nature; in fairness the symbolism was not lost on him! Nonetheless the whole episode exemplified a wider breakdown in relationships and partnerships. Ministers no longer even appeared to listen, or felt a need to compromise or explain. By the mid-1990s this had become their universal practice. In the aftermath of Baker's decision the teachers staged strikes and work-to-rule. ACAS, the independent arbitration body, was called in to mediate, and I was appointed to assist them. It was a wonderful experience, the final step in honing negotiating skills and exercising insights into human nature and aspirations. We succeeded in finding a compromise. I was almost sorry when it was over; I had been extended to the limit, and I had enjoyed every moment of it!

Burnham was abolished when it should have been reformed. One positive achievement survived in the form of teacher appraisal.

CHAPTER FOURTEEN

Teacher Appraisal

WHILE in Suffolk I became involved in the question of how teachers' classroom performance could be assessed with a view to improving standards. The events which followed spanned my time in Suffolk, in Humberside and later at the NCC. To tie the threads together, and at the cost of anticipating a few events, I have, as it deserves, put the tale in a chapter of its own between my sojourns in Suffolk and Humberside.

I've no idea who 'Burnham' was, but his committee which negotiated teachers' salaries in the annual round, occasioned me many late nights, and the teaching profession in England and Wales, many sleepless ones in the 1980s. It is never wise to miss meetings at which jobs are being allocated, but I was not present when it was agreed to set up a group to investigate the merits of instituting a system of teacher appraisal. I was the unanimous choice, in absentia, for this unglamorous task. Looking back I can see that fate had caught up with me. Ever since my visit in the late 1970s to Boston to recruit teachers for Strathclyde, a question put to me by applicants from all over the States had troubled me. To a man (and woman) they asked about the frequency and nature of 'competence checks' on performance in the UK. Open incredulity greeted my response that from the training college cradle, to the retirement grave, no formal check was made on the work of a teacher. Some of our American recruits no doubt came just because of this significant omission, most simply shook their heads in rank disbelief. From that time on, every time I raised the question of appraisal, it was met on both sides of the Border with reactions ranging from indifference to open hostility — not least from my own father, who took the extreme view that as a trained professional, only the teacher could decide what went on in the classroom, and that without outside interference. He failed to recognise that while the most skilled in any job, as he assuredly was, could soldier on on their own, others could not and needed support, training, and occasionally to be shown the door.

In short there was a conspiracy of silence about teacher competence — as indeed there was, at that time, about doctors and lawyers too. Dismissal for incompetence was virtually unknown, and often those doing most damage to children were promoted by 'golden references' to get rid of them. Often dishonest, these were at best ambiguous, like the one I saw in Suffolk which concluded with the enigmatic, 'The school which gets this teacher to work for them will be fortunate indeed'! I remembered too that when in Suffolk we had decided that some of our poorest teachers and heads had to go, almost all of them had said, 'If only someone had been honest with me in the past' and then confessed to some relief that the pretence was over. I was equally aware that praise was at a premium for teachers. There was no machinery for saying to the good unsung teacher 'well done, thou good and faithful servant.' This was brought home to me when in Kansas City I was invited to make awards to 100 teachers selected by their schools for their care of handicapped pupils. The school board booked the Hilton, gave their whole families lunch, and after a photo-call each was presented with an ornately framed citation, which I read before presenting it to them. The look in their eyes and those of their families said it all.

What was to be done? The mere establishment of the appraisal committee led to the predictable polarisation of views. Politicians hailed the opportunity at last to fire the vast army of lazy leftie layabouts littering our schools with long holidays and short hours. Union extremists said that it was simply a witch-hunt to de-stabilise an excellent teaching force, with 'employers' narks' spying on impeccably industrious practitioners. The stage was set, the challenge clear.

There was no prospect of agreement to trial a system at national level, but such was the level of trust in Suffolk that teachers' leaders, with adequate safeguards about the anonymity of the guinea pigs, were willing to co-operate. The result was a government grant which, thanks to the ability of the senior civil servants to handle ministers, was given to enable us to find the middle road — helpful and supportive to teachers, but with sufficient teeth to compel improvement. We were to examine the systems then in use in the private and public sectors, and the teacher-appraisal schemes in Germany, Canada and the USA. A small team was set up with three seconded heads in the front line: Ken Green, Wilf Horsfield and Margaret Sanders.

We reeled round the Armed Services, the Civil Service, Shell, IBM, Boots and Marks and Spencer, imbibing their corporate hospitality. We learned that unless the process is respected by those being appraised, it is lost, and can all too easily be taken to the cleaners. There has to be 'something in it' for both sides, employer and employee. Much of what we observed was mechanistic and examined tangible things only — the easily measurable, the conventional. Memories of 'Bawdsey Bill' flooded into my mind. We saw little which we could equate with what goes on in the classroom.

We packed our toothbrushes, renewed our passports and set off for foreign climes. In Germany we made little progress. German teachers are civil servants and are treated accordingly. We were told: 'Evaluation of teachers in Germany is a bureaucratic irrelevance; they have jobs for life, cannot be dismissed or made redundant however bad their appraisals.' Not surprisingly appraisal was mechanistic, irregular and ineffective. If we had none, they had a system just as ineffective but much more costly.

From Germany we flew across the Atlantic to London, Ontario. I can remember how brown and compressed the ground was. It was the early Spring, the deep snow had melted away, but no life had returned to the soil. The welcome was warm, and what we saw was encouraging. Teachers there clearly believed in appraisal, set themselves goals, and were evaluated on these by colleagues they trusted. The sting was in the tail — everybody was appraised, including the director of education, and teachers could say openly what they thought of her performance. This was demonstrably fair, but I could not help wondering what teachers might say in England about some of the stuffier education chiefs, not to mention that Scottish oddball in Suffolk!

Across the border we went into the States, where in education you can see every contrast known to man and a few more besides. We flew to Washington where I found that I was the only one in the group prepared to drive a rather large Pontiac — left-hand drive and automatic — through the rush-hour. After an hour, during which we aged perceptibly we finally made it to the sanctuary of our hotel only to find it was overbooked. We found respite in an apartment which turned out to be a centre for the drug trade, and a base for prostitutes. We received some very sporting offers both by phone and via the letter-box and had to sit up all night to protect the honour of our lady group-member.

Next day I attended a Rotary Club meeting in the most affluent golf and country club in Washington. The meal was served by tail-coated flunkeys resplendent in red, and was followed by a trip to the locker-room where the respectability (as far as I could see) of the massage-parlour contrasted neatly with the experiences of the night before. One member owned the up-market hotel beside the airport, and promised to fix us up with rooms for the night. He did: a penthouse suite on the top floor with panoramic views, lounges, dedicated staff, and meals at our own table. We were terrified; what would it cost? Would a spy from the *Daily Mirror* expose our luxury life at taxpayers' expense? Despite the stunning views of the Potomac, the magnolia and the blossoms in bloom — Spring had sprung — we spent our second sleepless night, by contrast in rooms haunted by opulence! I had looked at the tariff behind the door, obligatory in American hotels, and could hardly count the 'nothings' after the dollar signs. At 8am our host arrived just as we had agreed to pay the bill from our own pockets. Bankruptcy loomed. 'It's on the house' was his opening remark! Boy did we then enjoy our breakfast of exotic fruits, lobster and waffles. I wish I could relive that whole experience, without the panic. The hotel's Cadillac took us to Arlington where we were to learn about another pitfall of appraisal, merit pay or payment by results, which had gone out in the UK in the 1890s. It did not take a millisecond to grasp how attractive this would be to Tory politicians

— not least Sir Keith Joseph, the Education Secretary, to whom the words appraisal and sacking sometimes appeared to be synonymous.

In 1985, in a suburb of Washington we found a prime example of something which besets our own nation ten years later. Payment by results may work for widget production; it certainly does not where human beings are the end-product. Whether it be a teacher required to produce examination results, or a chief constable tasked to arrest more criminals, it only works if the goals and aims are agreed and the complexity recognised. Every complex problem has a simple solution and it is wrong. If agreement is not reached, the ill-will generated is counterproductive and the system is subverted. In Arlington it had been decided that 'excellent' teachers would get $1,000-a-year bonus and 'very good' ones $750. The 'quota' was 100 of each. Bedlam ensued. What were the definitions of 'excellent' and 'very good'? Soon everyone was bending the rules. At the end of a year those judged 'excellent' were pleased, if mystified, but the 'very good' were livid! Why were they not 'excellent'? Human nature being what it is, they seemed more resentful than if they had missed out on the rewards altogether. We left Arlington convinced that crude incentives did not work. We were amused to hear of a neighbouring school board which had decided to grade administrative staff as 'excellent', 'very good' and 'good'. They omitted to cash-limit the experiment. At the end of the first year 10% were adjudged excellent, 15% very good and 10% good. Three years later 60% were excellent, 40% very good and none were simply good. They drew lots each year for the 'excellent' and 'very good' bonuses. They earned our total respect — full marks for playing the system.

We did see in Fairfax County, another suburb of Washington, a rather good 'Teacher Incentive Plan' (no mention of merit) where teachers themselves applied for recognition and, if they got it and the extra $1,000, had to be reassessed every three years. But of course, many good teachers were too modest to apply.

In Fairfax we came across other questions, for example should pupils be able to give views on teachers — why not? Should the staff of the school be able to appraise their head? In the words of one teacher I met, 'It sure as hell would lose credibility if the principals and superintendents were not evaluated.' It was the same teacher who introduced me to NETMA: nobody ever tells me anything. Appraisal can lead to criticism of bosses as well as workers, and this is no bad thing.

At this point one of my companions, Ken Green, evoked a strong desire to visit relatives in Georgia, 'just down the road'. Fatally, I did not look at the map and was prevailed upon to accompany him. At the obligatory 55mph it took a day and a bit to get there, in sweltering heat. Ken was not a popular man. In fairness he did take us to dine in a Pullman car marooned in the middle of what looked like a cotton plantation, where the magnificent Kentucky chicken owed nothing to Colonel Sanders. What was surprising was the evident poverty of many black people living in shacks and huts by the roadside. What a contrast to well-heeled Fairfax and Arlington.

At least this vast detour afforded an excuse on the way back to cross Chesapeake Bay which is spanned by more than 20 miles of alternating tunnels and bridges with restaurants on 'islands' affording spectacular views. Now if only the Channel Tunnel had been built like that, how much more fun it would be to travel to Europe. On the other side of the bay we stayed in a hotel in the most idyllic of settings. I was so overcome by a feeling of well-being that as I reclined in the communal jacuzzi in the company of three rather pleasantly shaped ladies, an involuntary remark that 'I felt like a new man' caused them to rise and leave in great haste.

Moving North to Greenwich, a leafy New England town, we managed to see it in its later-than-Washington springtime. We were met by the superintendent of the school board, a tall affable man, who looked and acted like James Stewart playing Walter Mitty. Such was his sense of direction that his staff were on stand-by to retrieve him from whatever part of the town he was lost in. We should have known when he drove us to a clam-bake at his favourite restaurant. After three cul-de-sacs, a supermarket car park, and a dead end at the river, we hailed a yellow cab which escorted us to our destination.

He was revered by his staff, but not for the appraisal system in operation. It was mechanistic and unfeeling and had been imposed without consultation. Teachers told us that as it had to be completed before Easter each year, by custom the last half-day of term was devoted to filling up the forms which were then filed for posterity. This was food for much thought; clearly a system which achieved results was not going to be easy to formulate. What did strike us forcibly was that teachers in Greenwich were well-paid, highly respected and valued by the community. They gave a lot in return, but on average achieved significantly less than their over-worked, underpaid colleagues in the UK. It is heartening to see nowadays the encouraging signs that parents and communities are more supportive of teachers, and 'teacher-bashing' by politicians has as a consequence diminished. Mark you, we are a long way from what I witnessed later in California. President Bush was present at a conference in person praising teachers and emphasising their value to the community. I felt weak at the knees — Margaret Thatcher was still prime minister then!

We returned to Suffolk to contemplate, to consult further and to produce a report which, despite my misgivings, was to be entitled 'Those having Torches', a quote from Plato's *Republic* which in full is 'Those having torches will pass them on to others'. It certainly stuck in the memory — 'Torches' for short. When I spoke about it at a national conference in Eastbourne, it was referred to inadvertently by another speaker as 'Those having Tortures'. Years later a friend who sought it out in the library of the Scottish Office found it not under Education, but in the Sociology Section under the title 'Those loving Touches'. I quite liked that.

When the team had produced the draft, with only a week to publication, I sat in a deck chair in my garden at Bucklesham and read it with mounting panic. Although the material was good, and the conclusions sensible, it was written in dreadful English, so jargon-ridden as to be incomprehensible to the average punter, and so naive that Sir Keith would have had it for breakfast. He would have to be led gently, if at all, to the conclusion that merit pay has its drawbacks. This sort of thing was to happen again and again at NCC. Clever, able people who had missed out on a disciplined education themselves when grammar grew unfashionable, knew nothing of sentence construction or the rules of parsing. Still less had they any political awareness or nous. They simply believed that if their case was strong, politicians must perforce accept it. 'Pull the other one' is the answer to that. In my experience a spot of pandering to prejudices, and a concealed message is the best hope that you have of winning them over.

As I sat down to rewrite 250 foolscap pages in 24 hours, I noticed one page where almost every sentence was followed with a bracketted credit like (Brown and Leggat, 1967) or (Allcock and Balls — *Psychology of the Newt,* 1976). This is how researchers gain credibility with each other, and publicise each other's obscure masterpieces. At last I found a sentence with no bracket and inserted the following: (Mills, *The Overlap Method,* 1981). It passed unchallenged the scrutiny of all the pundits, one or two of whom gratifyingly claimed to have read it! It was in fact a reference to Mick Mills, the Ipswich Town skipper and full back whose overlapping down the wing had done much to help the Portman Road team win the UEFA Cup. You've got to watch those academics.

The final product, christened with unintentional accuracy by the education press as the 'Graham Report', was considered clear, lucid, and realistic. It earned me the rare, if dubious, accolade of praise from both sides of the House of Commons — 'a distinguished gentleman' said Giles Radice. 'Very distinguished,' added Chris Patten. The report's conclusions form the basis of the successful system now compulsory in every English and Welsh school today. In truth they were no more than applied common sense. A scheme to succeed had to command the respect of teachers, both in its methods, including classroom observation, and in the calibre of the assessors. Its aim should be to improve competence, and foster self-confidence. Above all it should not be crudely linked to dismissal of teachers, or to promotion and cash. Clearly there would be something wrong if those who got very poor reports went on teaching regardless, or if the outstanding did not gain due advancement. A follow-up, inevitably 'In the Light of Torches', was published in 1987.

The report was accepted by the secretary of state, who asked for trials in six LEAs, and that particular attention be paid to the appraisal of head teachers, of whom Sir Keith said 'Good head teachers are the nearest thing we have to a magic wand.' Mark you, he almost brought the whole process to an end by what came to be known as his 'Hanging and Flogging' speech. I heard it on the *Today* programme on Radio 4 as I was shaving — just as well it was a safety razor! In one of his periodic drifts to the right — occasioned when he allowed his great intellect to divert him — he had cut loose the previous evening and assured a political gathering that the real purpose of appraisal was firing the incompetent forthwith if not fifthwith. His concealed motives all-too-clearly revealed, he provoked a teacher boycott which took literally two years of patient reassurance to overcome. Union militants had a field day, and the sensible men of the National Union of Teachers, men such as Peter Griffin, Alan Evans, and Doug McEvoy, deserve medals for their efforts to reopen the debate, as did John Wiggins, the civil servant who helped to reassure successive secretaries of state. I saw Sir Keith privately a few days after his outburst. Head in hands he looked, and no doubt was, a picture of abject repentant misery. 'Public servants such as yourself have enough to do without interference from me,' he lamented. I was torn between kicking him and consoling him. He was too nice and genuine a man to be angry with for long. I wish some of his successors could have been more sensitive to the role of public servants.

Kenneth Baker, who succeeded Sir Keith as Secretary of State for Education, was positively in favour of appraisal. In the course of my work with him on the curriculum, I had the opportunity to keep him abreast of the work of the Appraisal National Steering Group which I chaired, and whose work had the backing of ACAS — the national arbitration service which had resolved so many union disputes over the years. Baker believed in the positive improvement of teachers' work, and could see that without overt crude links, some of what his right-wingers were pressing for could be achieved. He promised his backing for the final report, and to press the treasury for the funds to pay for appraisal — a tiny percentage of the overall teachers pay budget. By this time appraisal of heads had been agreed, not without great shenanigans, as their leaders claimed that sauce for the goose was quite a different recipe from sauce for the gander — full marks for ingenuity. An unconvincing claim that only heads could appraise heads was rightly ridiculed by rank and file teachers, and we were ready for action. Almost four years' work had at last borne fruit, and for the first time in living memory — literally — every one of the six teacher unions, including the 'difficult' National Association of Schoolmasters, was in full agreement with their local authority employers. All that remained was for the secretary of state to put pen to paper.

On 25th July, 1989, Kenneth Baker was summoned before the prime minister and offered the poisoned chalice of the party chairmanship. Many consequences were to follow from that fateful appointment by a lady who seemed to be harbouring dynastic ambitions — only a couple of months earlier she had appeared on the steps of Number 10 proclaiming, 'We have become a grandmother of a grandson.' She appointed John McGregor as Secretary of State for Education, news which was eclipsed by the dismissal of Geoffrey Howe as Foreign Secretary.

Civil servants and my own staff at the NCC were agog with speculation about the new man at Elizabeth House. It soon became clear that he was a pleasant, conscientious man, who felt that Baker had pushed too far too quickly on a whole range of educational policies. Perhaps like others he felt that Baker had once again escaped the consequences of his actions — a bit unfair, as Baker later told me that he had genuinely wished to remain in education. Within a week, civil servants were telling me that McGregor intended to win teacher support by hauling back on new initiatives, and allowing 'breathing space'. With the unerring skill which only politicians possess, he had selected teacher appraisal for postponement.

I rushed to see him and was courteously received. As we stood in his office high above Waterloo Station, looking across at the Thames, and the former Clyde steamer *Queen Mary*, moored at the embankment, he told me that he was postponing appraisal for six months 'in order to allow consultation with industry'! I showed him a list from 'Torches' of the 31 leading companies who had already been involved and given their support, but in vain. He had picked the wrong pretext for delay, but the outcome would be the same. He seemed patently frightened too of the treasury — as a former chief secretary there, he was reluctant to go back cap-in-hand, pleading. He knew, by his own admission, nothing about the education service, and was therefore quite unable to grasp the unique significance of agreement by all the teacher unions on anything — not least appraisal. A priceless chance was lost; he had drawn back from the one thing teachers had agreed to accept, and of course pressed on with things they regarded as a waste of time. My frustration was total. After a polite chat and a cup of tea, I left desolate and in despair — I look forward to reading John

McGregor's memoirs if they are ever published. Will he be able to recognise a lost opportunity in retrospect?

His successor, who accepted little advice from me, or indeed anyone else, was receptive to the idea of appraisal. He formally opened the NCC headquarters in York in 1990, three days after he had succeeded John McGregor as Secretary of State. I remember the occasion only too well. We had a stone inscribed heavily with his predecessor's name for him to unveil! The stonemasons of York worked round the clock to erase one Secretary and inscribe another. Would that politician's deeds were as easily obliterated! Clarke over lunch assured me that he had not asked McGregor what was going on in education, and implied that he intended to 'change everything on principle'. Such is continuity between Tory ministers. While the news was bad for the curriculum, logically it should be good for appraisal. By the cheese and biscuits, washed down with a first-class Gevrey-Chambertin he was convinced that the appraisal scheme should be disinterred and given new life.

The scheme remained as sound as ever, but the results were affected by his general attitude to teachers, and by starving it of funds, lumping the costs on to hard-pressed local authorities and individual school budgets. Where it has worked well it has achieved its objectives and more. Where it is most needed in less efficient schools, it has been side-stepped and downgraded. Shades of Greenwich in Connecticut. Still, at its worst it must be better than the latest wheeze of the Government — that on four-yearly (soon to be six-yearly) inspections of schools, teachers should be classified on grades one to seven on the strength of one or two observed lessons with those rating six and seven more or less shown the door! That is summary justice on the grand scale. I look forward to the cases of wrongful dismissal which will for sure reach industrial tribunals in great numbers.

My time in Suffolk was drawing to a close. At the age of 50, I had to decide between ten more delightful years there, or a new challenge. I was anxious to test the theory that the chief executive of a major county need not be, as traditionally, a lawyer or an accountant. While this may have served in the days when the county clerk was largely a figurehead and departments such as highways, education and social services went their own ways, in the new corporate era it seemed to me that a 'front-line' man had much to offer. No chief education officer had become chief executive of an English county. It was time to take the plunge.

Donald Miller was heading for the fate of his predecessors as I began to fill in the application form for Humberside. In his own constituency of Southwold, there was a tiny secondary school at Raydon, which was hopelessly unviable educationally, and also too many primary schools. In spite of his experience, he believed that the folks there would listen to reasoned argument, appreciate the need for change, and accept his proposals. They didn't. He lost his seat on the council, and his chance of being chairman of the county council. Democracy can be cruel. In his tolerant way he forgave them, but it was no surprise to read of his death a few years later. In their different ways Richard, Felicity and Donald had fought the good fight. They understood the value of everything, not the price of nothing.

PART IV

Humberside

The Humber Bridge

THE post of chief executive of a county council was created as part of the restructuring of local government on both sides of the border in 1974. Corporate management was all the rage. In essence all the disparate functions of local government from highways to libraries, from trading standards to education were to be brought together to achieve coherence and cohesion. 'To what end?', traditionalists queried. It was too late for rational argument: what had been found good for commercial conglomerates in the USA in the 1960s (and since abandoned) was to be good for local government. Now chief officers of all departments would form a management team to be presided over by the chief executive. Unlike the amiable county clerks of the past, such as Charlie Ross in Renfrewshire, the new breed was much more than 'primus inter pares'. He was to be 'first' and the rest were not to be 'equals'. There was some merit in reducing duplication and fostering a one-door approach for the convenience of ratepayers, but the cost was to tie up chief officers for hour after hour, ostensibly bringing together services with little or nothing in common. In Suffolk I had spent 15% of my week in such meetings and often much less in schools.

Most of those appointed in the first wave in 1974 were existing clerks — old and almost invariably lawyers, occasionally treasurers. Whatever their talents, they tended to lack front-line experience.

THE ROBERT OPIE COLLECTION

at the

MUSEUM OF ADVERTISING & PACKAGING

GLOUCESTER

THE ALBERT WAREHOUSE
GLOUCESTER DOCKS · GLOUCESTER GL1 2EH
Telephone: **(0452) 302309**

A NOSTALGIC JOURNEY

In the heart of historic Gloucester, you can experience a nostalgic journey back through the memories of your childhood, all brought vividly to life again by the Robert Opie Collection.

The result of one man's enthusiasm, Britain's first museum of advertising and packaging is the culmination of over 25 years' research and collecting by Robert Opie. His Collection, the largest of its type in the world, now numbers some 300,000 items relating to the history of our consumer society. It provides a fascinating insight into the British way of life over the past hundred years.

Here they all are, the packs, tins and bottles which filled the larder and added flavour to family mealtimes, the posters and display cards which enlivened the corner shop, the popular cigarette brands, the favoured patent medicines, and the enamel signs which brought colour to shops and railway stations.

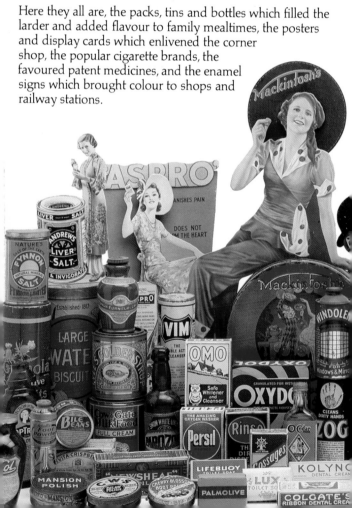

They were cautious, seeing every penny of the ratepayers' money as their own, and more attuned to the 'game' of county hall than the problems of rural schools or the need to start change from where things were, rather than form a corporate master plan. Clifford Smith in Suffolk was not only the first but one of the best and most far-seeing of them, but even he lacked the experience which day-to-day contact with a major service brings. Recognising this, he encouraged me to put to the test the theory that a front-line chief officer with the largest local service as his responsibility could do a better job. We both recognised the difficulty which would be posed by 'breaking the mould'. Most senior councillors were comfortable with legal or financial expertise to hand, as distinct from management know-how. They regarded educationalists with suspicion. Their claims to be 'different', their idealism, their obsession might make them unable to be dispassionate in allocating budgets. Could group leaders accept the counter argument that empathy with other service chiefs would help them to lead without dictating? The time had come to test the theory and the water.

Fate cast up the turbulent waters of the Humber Estuary which divided the two disparate parts of the hybrid Humberside created in 1974. It embraced the East Riding of Yorkshire from Bridlington to Hull and inland to Beverley and the Wolds, all north of the Humber, and North Lincolnshire to its south (if you see what I mean!) — Grimsby, Immingham, Cleethorpes on the coast, Goole and Scunthorpe inland. Across the river and between the cultures lay the Humber Toll Bridge. It was the most expensive toll bridge in England — at that time more than £2 for a single crossing. Instead of a symbol of unity, it had became a totem of frustration and division. Campaigned for by Barbara Castle in the 1960s, it was seen by the Tories as a 'Labour bridge' and treated accordingly.

Looking forward a bit, I can recall the day when Peter Bottomley, then transport minister, and as yet much better known than his wife Virginia, visited the bridge. Patiently, I explained to him that if Humberside was to have any chance, the tolls would have to go and the accumulating debts be written off. He regarded me with that amused contempt that was fast becoming the hallmark of government ministers, and replied, 'You are lucky to have a bridge at all.' There was no polite answer to that. What a pity he clipped his limousine on a bollard as he roared off to talk down to the natives in Hull!

In blissful ignorance of the problems, I sent off to county hall in Beverley for the details of the post. Back they came with the information that the county was politically perfectly 'hung' — 36 Labour, 36 Tory, and 4 Liberals (as they then were). It was not pointed out that the Liberals, led by the redoubtable John Bryant, were hopelessly split and liable to tie 2-2 in crucial votes! More ominously there had been no chief executive for about three years. Labour (in control then) had dispensed with his services on the basis that he was an expensive luxury — presumably he had sat on some of their more extreme mad-cap schemes. The resultant chaos — a headless corporate chicken with chief officers and committee chairmen roaming like robber barons of old, had convinced the other two parties of the need to reinstate the post. It was not made clear that the Labour hierarchy, headed by Terry Geraghty, were only co-operating under duress and would give the new incumbent anything but a smooth ride. Even so it did not take much reading between the lines to see the challenge which lay ahead. To me it was irresistible, provided the ground rules were clear, not least a five-year cast-iron contract with full compensation for an enforced 'early bath'. In spite of the drawbacks a high-class field was assembled, and I was surprised to make the short list, more so to be offered the job. A gloomy prognostication from the treasurer, a disappointed candidate, that they would 'get me' only added to the fun, and sadly indicated that I could expect trouble from that quarter. He had pictures of steam trains all round his room — sometimes a bad sign in my experience, an 'anorak' being an uncomfortable thing when worn over a pin-striped suit, if you see what I mean.

Three months later I took up residence in my caravan at a holiday site in Bridlington, to be followed by the family to a new house in North Dalton three months later. It created quite a stir on the site on the occasions when the official Daimler with the chairman's pennant flying called to collect me for formal dinners. This was not an infrequent occurrence as, in total contrast to Suffolk, Humberside did itself proud. The chairmen behaved like Lord Mayors — they had Jaguars as well as Daimlers, a well-stocked booze-cabinet, and each an entourage of three flunkeys to minister to his needs. Unfortunately the chief of these had just been suspended pending prosecution for confusing the county's liquid assets with his own. The chairman was an old-time Tory councillor, a delightful and sympathetic man whose support I came greatly to value. He was a canny manipulator with a 'butter wouldn't melt in my mouth' technique. Small and dapper, the twinkle in his eye and his talent for irreverent asides made the interminable dinners which were almost a weekly occurrence more bearable. I and my wife were expected to attend all these glittering occasions.

I am to this day allergic to formal dinners and avoid them like the plague. To sit down between two ladies abandoned by their husbands for the evening and keep the social banter going for up to three hours, non-stop, with only the deadly *bon mots* of the speakers to look forward to, requires talent and stamina beyond reason. I vividly recall the night sandwiched between a sad Japanese lady with fractured English, but loquacious, and a Labour lady from Hull who suspected that her other or better half was enjoying a more than platonic relationship with one of my economic development officers. When the head waitress (a relative of a leading councillor) splashed soup on my dinner jacket with more than her usual abandon, I fled to the gents for, and with, great relief. When I returned the ladies were discussing the relative merits of mistresses and geisha girls with singular intensity. A gentleman to the core, I changed seats to let them sit together. I found myself thus next to the region's beauty queen, but got little more out of her than Michael Aspel used to in those gripping interviews in Miss World contests. She was however, decidedly easy on the eye.

I began to appreciate just how my predecessor had felt the strain. The ceremonial life, with my presence obligatory, could have been a full-time remit on its own. Getting the precedence wrong on a table plan could have more immediately dire consequences than having a school burned down by arsonists — so easily can all sense of priorities become distorted when the county hall 'game' is in full swing. If only we could have devoted all of our time to internal politics and junketing. I am even now reminded of the celebrated *Yes, Minister* episode in which a new and fully-staffed hospital functioned perfectly without the inconvenience of having any patients.

This feeling was compounded during twinning trips abroad where you could find two sets of politicians celebrating a liaison which had not the slightest relevance either to the workers of, say, Cleethorpes or the hapless citizens of an obscure town in Westphalia. Perhaps they had it right in junket-free Suffolk, I mused on one such visit where, after a flight in a small plane during which the pilot served the drinks while the plane flew itself, we arrived at the height of the asparagus season. Every one of the seven banquets given in our honour featured my favourite vegetable. Unfortunately asparagus was not the staple diet of the Labour group on the council, and we only just avoided a major incident with our lot outraged at being subjected to such inedible rubbish and our hosts irate at their *pièce de résistance* being pushed aside with all-too-obvious signs of distaste. Only during the growing season in Spain in recent winters have I had such a gourmet's treat, but at least in Garrucha I am never alone in my appreciation. As we clambered back aboard our micro-jumbo, Terry Geraghty emaciated and starving, our hosts presented each of us with a beautifully wrapped parcel of asparagus in addition to the customary flags and paperweights — the discarded parcels at Humberside International Airport filled half of our freezer at home!

All this was fun, provided one's sense of humour and of the ridiculous could be sustained, but it had little to do with the grim reality of a county in crisis, demoralised and badly needing leadership and inspiration. Why, with a precious sense of timing, the royal family should decide on 13 formal visits to Humberside in my 18 months there is a question worthy of erudite research. The consequences I cover in a chapter of their own. As it was, the gulf between reality and county hall was widening daily as I had to wrestle with decisions affecting nearly a million souls and 44,000 staff while attending meetings with the chairman, a somewhat distrait lord lieutenant, and a prickly chief constable to decide life and death issues such as who took precedence in the queue to shake hands with the Princess of Wales on the tarmac at Humberside airport.

Problems and Solutions

THE real problems in Humberside were obvious. For me they ranged from the disaffection of the populace, to hot potatoes such as whether Nirex nuclear waste material should be dumped in the county, to a workforce of 44,000 souls ill-prepared for the massive changes which the Government's open tendering and privatisation policies made inevitable. There was bound to be a seismic culture shock in an authority where preserving the jobs of dinner ladies was unquestioningly accepted as being more important than providing books and jotters in schools. More immediately, the room occupied by my hapless predecessor had been half-inched by the Conservative group, and the alternatives suggested were calculatedly down-market.

A quick tour of HQ in Beverley revealed a dignified red-brick building of some age, with the usual mixture of annexes ancient and modern behind. There was an elegant council chamber with stained-glass windows where I would soon learn that meetings could be long, invariably shedding more heat than light, and where intervals were allowed for the procurement and consumption of fish and chips.

The view which greeted the casual visitor to county hall was appalling — a seedy entrance with a huge press office on the left (we had more staff than the local paper!), and a ghastly Letraset board with the day's business on it — entries largely misspelled. Education notices were particularly prone to howlers. What might once have been a dignified stairway to the council chamber had the dirtiest run-ner-carpet I'd ever seen. Here was a multi-million-pound enterprise with a sorry image even by Suffolk standards — at least everything looked cared for at county hall in Ipswich.

My next surprise was to find that two-thirds of the main building appeared to be assigned to party offices, staffed by a complete paid entourage devoted to partisan business at the ratepayers' expense. Each of the three leaders had a commissariat headed by a PA/secre-tary of awe-inspiring status. Such apparatchiks invariably ape the attitudes of their masters and the Labour dragon's kindly offer to try to 'fit me in for a few minutes in a day or so' was mind-boggling con-sidering she was in theory a member of my staff! On that basis I might get to see Terry Geraghty, the leader in a week or two. The Liberals had a small and remote eyrie, littered with out-of-date man-ifestos and dirty coffee cups. Even so, it was bigger than all the rooms occupied by the councillors in Suffolk. The councillors representing the major parties had all the creature comforts of a good hotel, and every incentive to 'live' in county hall. As I have said, for the chief executive not even a room, never mind a secretary, although there was a helpful suggestion that the leader's number two would 'do' for me when time permitted. No doubt her duties could include a photo-copy of all my correspondence for Labour files.

The gauntlet had been thrown down; if I were to achieve anything 'out there' county hall would have to be sorted out first even if it meant the 'game' rather than the reality. A word with caretakers and the cleaners was in order. I soon found a magnificent room earmarked for annexation by the Labour group who in turn would pass on some space to the Tories. It had an antique fireplace, some fine furniture, and it afforded what estate agents (and the Tory Leader Alec Ramshaw was one) describe as 'scope for development'. Next door was part of the PR empire which could be adapted as an 'outer sanctum'. Some weeks later I moved in to what was at least a match for the politicians' suites, not because I have ever hankered for the magnifi-cent — that weakness usually afflicts chief constables in my experi-ence — but to make a point which had to be made. I had appointed only one personal assistant but she matched in rank that of both Labour and Tory leaders and was considerably shrewder. I leave you to imagine for yourself what had happened behind the scenes while all this was achieved. Much blood was spilled on council carpets, and it wasn't mine. Ominously, the necessary authorisations were voted through by Tory and Liberal with Labour abstaining. Open hostility was beginning, however, to mellow into grudging respect. If you've roughed it in Gorbals, you are well prepared for what the natives of Hull (or 'ull as they pronounced it) can throw at you.

As part of the new image we modestly refurbished the entrance hall, installed TV screens for the day's business, (à la Palace of Westminster) and put a proper carpet on the stair to the council chamber. Press reports influenced by the two factions in our press office ranged from 'profligate waste of ratepayers' money' to a 'timely restoration of a tarnished image'. Estimated costs of the carpet ranged from a few pounds a square yard to over £30. The fact that it was the former was largely ignored. Carpets can be political dynamite. Years later when I was working in York for the NCC, the builders of our new HQ took it upon themselves to lay a carpet containing the NCC logo at their own expense. Soon the popular dailies were lambasting me for spending countless thousands on plush carpets while schools were falling down through lack of cash. Nobody wanted to hear the truth — the story was too emotive and too good for that.

It was time to find out more about the key players in the soap opera that was Humberside, both chief officers and politicians. I soon found that I could not meet the county architect. He had been suspended on charges relating to what belonged to him and what to the authority. He was to be found not guilty many months later, but his department was demoralised with bitter debate as to whether he could ever credibly return to his post. I could have done without all this, not least because this was an area where I suspected maximum political penetration and influence over decisions and staff. In the end I took the considerable gamble of appointing Mike Pitt, Deputy Highways Director, to the post, the gamble lying only in his discipline of engineer rather than architect. He was a superb officer who fully justified my faith in him, and in time proved again that chief executives could come from service departments when he became Chief Executive of Cheshire County Council. Not least of his achievements in

Humberside was to release talented architects from the dull conventions of local government design with results clearly and beneficially to be seen in the towns and villages of the county.

John Moore, the Highways Director, was a delightful and loyal colleague who initiated me into the mysteries of his craft. For years he had been locked in friendly combat with his opposite number in North Yorkshire to have the best surfaces where their roads met at county boundaries. The latter probably had the edge in one respect. He it was who adorned the entrance to every village with these lovely stone mill-wheels which bear the community's name — a lovely and enduring touch for native and visitor to enjoy. John Moore was an adept manipulator of politicians, and in time became my deputy. He fought a long and unavailing campaign for an East-coast motorway to relieve the ghastly congestion on the A1, and to give belated purpose to the Humber Bridge. He and we lost, partly because of the 'green' lobby but more I suspect because the Humber was a 'Labour bridge'. I wonder still what relative damage a road, avoiding the sensitive Wolds and the Yorkshire coast, and linking Cambridge with Teesside would have done. Try a rush-hour trip on the A1 if you want to see the cost of that opportunity missed.

Nowhere in Humberside was my arrival greeted with more apprehension than in the education service. I like to think that some forward-looking teachers hoped that a rather stodgy service, sound but uninspiring, might take off as Suffolk had. From the Director of Education and his staff came understandable vibes of apprehension of a take-over from the top. I had made a vow, to which I managed to stick with difficulty, not to interfere in my first love beyond the legitimate interests of my post. Where I got involved was when 'economies' were called for and the priorities were, as I hinted earlier, distorted by political considerations — non-teaching jobs or text books. The first of many consultants called in to tell us the obvious reported that we had 186 kitchens too many for our needs! The director, long in the tooth, was powerless in the face of his chairman, the redoubtable Max Bird, an ambitious and articulate politician with an eye to the populist vote. Nor could he hope to stand up to the Tory education leader, Professor Arthur Pollard, whose views on education tended to make Genghis Khan look like a woolly liberal, and who had the ear of the right-wing clique causing so much trouble nationally to Keith Joseph and later Kenneth Baker. The phrase 'political football' aptly summed up the state of education as Max and Arthur slugged it out. I found both congenial company and did what I could behind the scenes.

Only the coming of a new director with talent and political acumen allowed the latent talent in Humberside to flower. The night before the interviews for the post I dined at the Pollard household and was privileged to watch the great man cut off in full flow by his charming wife. A disadvantage of marrying a young and gifted student is the risk of having intellectual rings run round you as the after-dinner mints are circulating. The next day Arthur, still fuming, made short shrift of the obligatory lady candidate on the short list, something which she was quite capable of doing for herself. How on earth did she succeed in being appointed to a similar post, before predictably joining the ranks of officers who found it wasn't after all a job for life?

After a time corporate management began to work in Humberside. I like to think that my years of experience in the front line made it possible to appreciate the problems and explore practical solutions. Certainly, I think, a beleaguered director of social services seemed relieved to find some support. With a budget out of control, fiddling rife in the outer reaches of the 'empire', and councillors fixing things for their mates, he did not have his troubles to seek. It is the fashion nowadays to knock social workers as a result of a few well-publicised disasters. In fairness 95 per cent of what they do is vital and effective. The other five per cent keeps the *Sun* and the *Daily Mirror* in business and social work chiefs awake at night wondering about child molestation and octogenerians being found tied to their beds by miserably-paid care assistants. As a society we lambast our chosen scapegoats all too readily. I fear that it's easier to do that than face up to the real costs of the standards we expect but refuse to pay for.

Sometimes in local government you come across a group of officers who seem to have 'gone native'. They think they are a cross between elected members and guardians of every penny in the public purse. Each penny spent on nurseries, old folks or street lighting is a failure on their part. They are nearly always treasurers (or in modern jargon directors of finance). As the social services department writhed in agony in Humberside, the treasurers stood in close attendance, ever ready to highlight shortcomings, expose incompetence, and suggest unworkable solutions.

When I wish to indulge in a rueful laugh about the folly of it all, I remember the case of the typist who left her bicycle in the section for motor cycles, from which it was duly stolen. Her claim for £27 compensation was dismissed by our eagle-eyed treasurer's department on the grounds that she had parked it in the wrong place. The unions complained, her colleagues protested, but the guardians of the public purse were immovable. The total cost of hearings, members' appeals panels, lawyers fees etc must have reached close on £2,000 before I managed to have a halt called. We'd have been better to buy the poor lass a second-hand Mini than to have gone on with the farce.

CHAPTER SEVENTEEN

Work and Play

DESPITE the distractions, I had to address the real problems faced by Humberside. To an extent these were the same as those faced by all local authorities in the late 1980s. Local government had become a convenient scapegoat for national politicians. From Michael Heseltine to Nicholas Ridley a succession of environment ministers imposed cut upon cut, blamed local authorities for the world's ills, and sought to reduce their role to that of a government contracting agency, privatising local services: responsibility without power. In vain did local councillors of all political hues try to defend their position. In a country without a written constitution, strength in the local areas is a necessary counterbalance to over-mighty national politicians and civil servants. Although demonstrably more efficient than government departments and agencies, the image of a handful of 'loony left' councils — the Liverpools, the Lambeths and the Brents — was cynically applied to over 500 hard-working authorities. The paradox was that this was a government which professed to a belief in local enterprise while being the most centralist of the century. While there is always a case for improving local authority standards, there is never one for central dictation, based on the prejudices of the 'Whitehall village'.

While even true-blue Tory shire counties were given short shrift, those of a redder hue were ruthlessly harried. One means of doing

this was to attack local authority officers as 'lefties' defending education and other services because of political opposition rather than to
safeguard quality. Alec Ramshaw, the Tory leader in Humberside was
so ashamed of his central office briefings that he used to show me
them. It was hard to recognise the folks I worked with as Marxist rev-
olutionaries, but that is how they were portrayed. Gone were the days
when councillors respected the views of their officers. Perhaps in the
1960s the great men of local government, the Alec Cleggs of Yorkshire
and the Hugh Fairlies of Renfrewshire, had been accorded too much
respect. If so, the tables had been well and truly turned. The demise
of the deference society meant that scant respect was paid to their
advice. I think it was Clausewitz who said that when a nation despises
its administrators it is dead.

As a result, the pressure was on, and nowhere more than in
Humberside, to force the suppression of unwelcome advice, and even
to 'doctor' committee papers to give the appearance of professional
approval for political sharp practice. I had a monumental struggle
insisting that while politicians could do what they wished with the
advice they were given, they could not then make public only the bits
which suited their pet schemes. In a county where committee papers
had been clearly 'got at' for three years, it was a daunting prospect.
Every day saw a battle of wills. Gone was the partnership which had
created the great and proud services in city and county. It became
harder to explain to sceptical teachers, social workers, road men and
librarians that politicians were indeed made aware by their officers of
the realities of every day life in the real world.

My supreme test came over, of all things, Hull Cricket Club. This
one-time bastion of Yorkshire at its best had fallen on hard times and
had been rescued by the council. While there was undoubtedly a real
will to see great matches once again on the hallowed turf, the club
and its bar had become a political home for the Labour group.
Malpractices ranged from naked nepotism in the appointment of bar
staff to using public funds for dubious projects. How the goings-on
escaped the tabloids was an abiding mystery. Attempts were made to
embroil me in the machinations — to condone them would have been
fatal. When the music stops and the roof falls in, it is usually the officer whom the auditors blame, while the politicians melt into the night.

Yet again a side-show was turning out to be more important than the needs of the people. It would have been only too easy to turn a blind eye and to enjoy the perks. Although I had never played cricket, I 'stood' as umpire in a match between Labour and a County XI, with no less a colleague than England's top umpire, Dickie Bird, at the other end. It was an unforgettable experience — not least as Terry Geraghty strode to the wicket, surveyed the field with disdain, adjusted his pads, twirled his bat and was plumb lbw first ball, even to my untutored eye! As I grappled with the enormity of the decision, and its consequences, Dickie Bird gave him out from square leg — perhaps the only instance of such a decision in the history of cricket. Geraghty's glare as he started the slow walk back, was met with the sunniest and most cherubic of Dickie's smiles. Rain stopped play before I had signalled too many wides as sixes, and he and I returned to the umpires' den to sup ale. I still treasure the pebbles which he gave me to help me count to six an over when play resumed.

The grudging respect which the Labour hierarchy were beginning to accord me was strained to breaking point by the symbolic clean-out of Hull Cricket Club which I perforce embarked upon. To their credit, they came to realise that if we worked together, many of their cherished dreams could be legitimately realised. Respecting their confidences, and those of the other parties, allowed me to find ways forward where once confrontation had been the order of the day. Although a Labour majority at the next triennial elections might still have led to the 'early bath' for me, we made progress. There were now occasions when, in my room, the leaders could compromise and co-operate behind closed doors. This would have been unthinkable six months before.

This growing tolerance was not allowed to surface in public. Committee meetings were played to the gallery with a ferocity which even now I find hard to believe. Personal abuse, fruity language, and challenges to 'meet outside' were occurrences, only the most extreme of which now roused the hardened press gallery from its slumbers. Barrack-room lawyers exploited every procedural device, and my knowledge of the rules of debate gradually became encyclopaedic. I frequently made up the rulings when to confess ignorance would have been fatal. As the standing orders ran to 30 pages of small print, it was a fair bet that the crises would pass before anyone had time to find the relevant bit.

Two of the debaters stand out from the rest, not least because there was between them a love-hate relationship based on an enduring double act. They grew to need each other and to respect each other. In the blue corner was the ebullient Betty Eaton, Tory lady extraordinaire. She was, literally, twice the woman that Felicity Cowley in Suffolk had been. Her picture hats were even broader and floppier, and she had the voice of a Billingsgate fishporter. In full flood, and she usually was, Betty could make the rafters ring and mix it with any man, matching expletive for expletive, without ever a trace of a blush. A heart of gold struggled with a fiendish sense of humour. I adored her!

In the red corner stood Charles Brady, long in the tooth, and being shouldered aside by the new Labour leaders. He was diminutive in stature, quiet of voice, and ever ready for a barney. He bated Betty and she knew and loved it. What would I give for a tape of their altercations. As MPs once used to gather in the House of Commons for the clashes between Gladstone and Disraeli, councillors and officers sped to the chamber when the news spread that they were 'at it again'. Out of the public eye they were the best of friends, and often found the way forward where their respective leaders had failed. Betty regretted the growing sway of the estate agents and small shopkeepers in Tory circles — pettifogging and visionless as they so often were. Equally Charles, a relic of the days when Labour took pride in service and 'the best for our people', secretly despised the ruling clique, telling me once that they were the very union leaders who'd brought Hull Docks to ruin with the rule book and restrictive practices and would, given the chance, do the same for Humberside. And well they might, if they had not been overtaken in turn by the young slick, well-educated and ambitious politicians already snapping at their heels. These were to provide more of a challenge to the established order than a demoralised Tory group, reduced to enjoying the perks without the power and a Liberal group who could not even decide what they were to be called — Liberal? Liberal Democrats? Social Democrats? Social Liberal Democrats? Democratic Liberals ... ?

Charles Brady's power base was the police committee — a body semi-independent of the county council, and which I served as 'Clerk to the Police Authority'. Of all the chief officers in local government, chief constables were the most to be envied. Once appointed their powers know few bounds. Not for them the petty constraints of politicians. Knowing that the Home Office alone could dismiss them — and wouldn't for fear of spoiling their image — they had it made. Wise ones concealed this, and made sure that they got on well with their committee. A few flattering words were usually enough to ensure their total support. The Chief Constable of Humberside was the exception. He elevated the parading of his power to an art form. He bullied, he lectured, he talked down to, and above all he patronised Charles Brady.

Charles did his best, advising tact, assuring the chief constable that no one in the committee was out to get him, and that his position would be more secure if he unbent a little. Then fate took a hand.

A young unemployed Labour councillor was openly despised by the chief. Not only had he long hair, and possibly a ring in his ear, he was gay. A few harmless questions about the police arsenal were so cuttingly dismissed, that the youth took to a chair in the library, called for every financial document he could find, and painstakingly compiled a complete costed shopping list of the weaponry in Humberside. I can't recall if it actually ran to bazookas, but it was pretty impressive, and led to some very pointed questions about what sort of 'operational matters' might lead to their deployment. It never pays to underestimate people. When Charles Brady retired, his parting gift to the chief was to have his gay protégé installed in his place.

Perhaps a more potent threat to the wellbeing of the natives of Humberside lay in the Nirex proposals to site a dump for low-level nuclear waste in Humberside's wilderness areas east of Hull or west of Grimsby. Humberside was on the short list and the idea was not popular with anyone. In addition to the natural 'why here' reaction, there was the feeling that all the places lucky enough to be considered were a good safe distance from Whitehall and Westminster. If all those nuclear things are so safe why have them in the extreme north of Scotland, on a remote Suffolk coast, or on the Welsh coast? A combination of environmentalists, CND and ordinary indignant folk saw them off — or seemed to. I suspect that they had simply decided that poor old Cumbria was a better bet. Sellafield was ultimately awarded the prize. Living in Cumbria as I now do, I was intrigued to learn recently that the abnormal number of leukaemia cases in the area is due not to Sellafield, but to faulty sewage disposal! This may explain why effluent from Sellafield can be traced drifting up the coast of Norway.

When I was in Suffolk, a remarkable incidence of cancer in children in Leiston, close to Sizewell, was dismissed as a statistical aberration. Nothing changes, as recent experiences with the causes of BSE have proved. Needless to say, seeing off Nirex was the pretext for yet another round of splendid dinners. No wonder I am allergic to dignitaries wearing chains of office — too much time spent, I suppose, fixing them to the loops which were sewn on to the shoulders of each new chairman's best suits.

The deliverance of the south bank of the Humber from Nirex led to an invitation to spend a day in Scunthorpe with its chief executive and an experience I won't easily forget. His pride and joy turned out to be the newly-opened crematorium. We must have a conducted tour. Nothing was spared behind the scenes — I had nightmares for days after peering into the furnaces at recognisable human remains not yet reduced to dust. The manager was a former rugby league player with the warmest of personalities, and real taste — only Richard Clayderman tapes were broadcast over the garden of remembrance.

By chance the next day I visited the chief executive of Hull, Basil Wood, who was soon to figure in a memorable royal episode. He explained to me that where I had gone wrong in Humberside was in not having a 'set of ermines' for formal occasions. No self-respecting chief executive should be without one. As I pondered the significance of this, he dived into a closet behind his desk to emerge a few minutes later in the complete works: red robes, trimmed in white ermine, garters like a bishop, and an absurd three-cornered, fur-trimmed hat. I was impressed, but hardly to the point of emulation. I laid aside the glossy catalogue he forced upon me with the alternative styles and prices. There was nothing off-the-peg; it was all made to measure. As events were to prove, such garments are not waterproof! It would have been reasonable to assume that there was more than enough lunacy around in Humberside to keep me fully occupied and amused without adding an external dimension. Returning from Basil's sanctum in Hull, I found on my desk a request to telephone the Department of Education about an invitation from Kenneth Baker to become a member of the National Mathematics Working Party — presumably on the basis that one member of this august body should be congenitally unable to add and subtract.

CHAPTER EIGHTEEN

The Mathematics Working Party

THE telephone call that was eventually to lead me away from Humberside came in the summer of 1987 to my office in Beverley and was from one of Her Majesty's Inspectors of Schools. The mathematics working group, she explained, would set out what every 5 to 16-year-old in every state school in England and Wales should know about mathematics, the first of the ten subjects to be tackled in the new national curriculum. These developments had rather passed me by, as you can imagine, and it struck me that this was a very tall order indeed. Kenneth Baker required a group of 15 or so, within just a year, to lay down the law (literally), and in the full glare of publicity, laced with political overtones.

Why me? Did they need an obligatory chief education officer to make up the numbers? Had they not noticed I had moved on from Suffolk? Worse still, had they mixed me up with the mathematician of the same name, author of many text books? Later confusion did once lead to my being introduced to a meeting in London as the 'eminent mathematician', a compliment, however wildly misdirected, which I have long cherished.

They were adamant; it was me they wanted. My political masters were initially happy to let me join. Some saw it as a compliment to

Humberside; others, I suspect, felt that they could well do without me for a couple of days a month. When I joined the group, chaired by Professor Roger Blin-Stoyle, at their second meeting in August 1987 they were already in considerable difficulty. They were old-guard educationists for the most part, accustomed to working groups that chatted for a couple of years before deciding to recommend nothing in particular. But this was for real: deliver by June 1988 — or else. Ignore the palpable hostility of the education establishment, make it simple, make it snappy, and, uniquely (then if not now) make it politically acceptable. In addition to the usual spread of educationists with views ranging from 'learning by enjoyment' to 'do your tables or else', there was a chap called Sig Prais who made it clear that he had been approached by Margaret Thatcher, a personal friend of his, to ensure that we got it right. Like the great lady herself, as I was to later learn, he did not go much for debate and compromise. He laid down how it had to be, and got pretty shirty if he did not get his way.

The chairman was clearly already out of his depth. The right, represented by Prais, resented the fact that recent improvements in maths teaching (and how they were needed!) were in danger of making it enjoyable. Sig did not buy that; he belonged to the school which believed that a thousand long divisions a day are somehow good for the soul, a kind of spiritual experience in their own right. Inevitably he saw calculators as a manifestation of evil, and wanted them banned to children until the age of 16. In vain did we tell him that any five-year-old could buy one in WH Smith for a few pounds.

The progressives, needless to say, were at the other extreme. To them long division and the learning of tables were no longer necessary. In any case much of this was 'too hard' for children and they should not be forced to do things. Indeed, unless a child enjoyed it it would have to go! Later two of the group threatened to resign when I suggested that there were some things in life you had to do, even though it hurt. They seemed to me to look forward to the day when children would be born with a calculator already grafted into their wrists. They most certainly did not believe in gain through pain.

The stage was set. I was inclined to the middle way, as I imagine most folks would be. Mathematics for me at school had been an abiding mystery. Why did people insist on filling their baths with the plugs out? Why were trains always rushing towards each other at combined speeds? Who really wanted to know the height of a flag-pole on top of a cliff? These were questions best left unanswered, along with sines and cosines. Like many of my generation, I wish that some time had been devoted at school to why things were so — learning through understanding. I passed in trigonometry but still didn't know for what useful purpose it exists.

On the other hand, I value highly competence at one's tables, and believe that it is important to be able to do long divisions, even if on most occasions nowadays one would use a calculator. Rote-learning has and always will have its place. Politically, I saw that we would both have to prevent mathematics heading back to Victorian times, and deter the lunatic left from destroying a disciplined approach. It was about this time, as I mentioned earlier, that a lady educationist from Oxford proposed the theory that children should learn to read by 'exposure to books', claiming that most of them would in time (presumably by osmosis) learn to read! No wonder the PM had sent her 'minder' along. Even Humberside's eccentrics appeared quite worryingly sane compared to this lot.

To say that the meetings in the autumn of 1987 were confused would be a gigantic understatement. The minutes of the previous meeting were usually totally rewritten, taking until lunchtime, following which some of the academics would hand round voluminous papers of their own, which the chairman added to the agenda without demur. I shall never forget one extended meeting at Stratford-upon-Avon where one learned professor brought his own computer, laid it on the table, and as the debate raged around him, typed in his instant views, printed them out and passed them round. What with these, and no less than four 20-page treatises handed out by other members, total chaos reigned. Kenneth Baker had required an interim report by November, and, fed the news of what was happening by his civil servants who surrounded us like clustering vultures, he let it be known that he was unimpressed, and that the whole thing was a conspiracy to hole his flagship national curriculum below the waterline. If it foundered at the first hurdle, to mix a metaphor, political oblivion awaited him.

In a frustrated kind of way I was quite enjoying it all. I contributed

manfully in the role of the man in the street — confessing to an ignorance of mathematics along with a worry about the future competi-
tiveness of our nation, and seeing it all as a glorious antidote to chief
constables, Labour leaders and crematoria visitations. On one occasion I admitted, to the evident surprise of the group, that I did not
possess a calculator and often did sums on the backs of envelopes
instead. They were so shaken that they had a whip-round and presented me with one — typically a model so complicated that it took
me ages to find even the on-off button.

Deep down I knew it could not go on, and speculated what Baker
would do to pull the fat out of his fire. I was attending the annual dinner of the Chief Executives' Society in the splendid premises of the
Law Society when I found out. I was accosted in the gents' loo by Sir
David Hancock, Permanent Secretary of the Education Department
— Baker's chief civil servant. No doubt you remember the first world
war recruitment poster in which Kitchener is pictured with his finger
pointing and underneath it states: 'Your country needs you.' He asked
me, point-blank, to take over as chairman. Blin-Stoyle had been fin-
gered, and would announce a diplomatic resignation in a few days.
The black spot was descending on me. I could refuse of course, but ...
There was I, fully stretched running a hung council, which was in
effect Labour-controlled, being asked to pull a Tory minister's chest-
nuts out of the fire.

I eventually decided I must go ahead with it — but for no more
than two days a month. I wonder what would have happened if I'd
said 'no', but when duty calls it's hard to refuse. I pay due tribute to
Humberside for co-operating. At least the news gave my father a good
laugh. A mathematician himself, he had about as little regard for my
ability in that field, as he had for the English as a nation. It confirmed
his worst suspicions about me and them!

The interim report received a hostile response from ministers and
the education establishment, Blin-Stoyle duly said his farewell piece,
and the gloves were off — six months left to do a job for which a year
had been deemed inadequate. We made it, but only just. Sig Prais
resigned at once making it clear that he didn't fancy working with me
one little bit. He apparently got a real ticking-off from Margaret
Thatcher who accused him of picking up his bat and walking away

from a sticky wicket — did she get her metaphors from Denis, I wonder? Baker helpfully stated that he did not want extreme solutions: 'I believe there is scope to find the right balance between the practice and mastery of basic skills, and the problem-solving approaches which have been introduced into our schools only during the last three or four years.' Showing a touching faith in yours truly, he said he was not so pessimistic as Sig Prais about our chances of success. Behind the scenes his civil servants roughed up some of the woollier members of the working group. They tightened their grip on our work — a move which I should have registered more clearly for the future than I did. In later years I was constantly at war with civil servants as they tried to have it all their own way.

For the time being, they were on my side. I met Kenneth Baker for the first time, but not the last, in his office high up in Elizabeth House with views across the Thames to the Houses of Parliament. We hit it off together, and he was open about his fears. The national curriculum, a cornerstone of his government's policy, hung by a thread. The consequences of failure could not be contemplated. Although personally fairly laid-back about the fate of the Thatcher, or indeed any, government, I formed the view, later confirmed, that Baker's heart was in the right place. I would do my best.

I invited anyone left in the working group who wanted to leave to do so. One or two shuffled their papers but no one made for the door. Next, I asked them to sign up formally to deliver the report on time. With that behind us, and a lecture on discipline — no re-runs of the minutes, no surprise papers, and no off-the-record comments to the press, we really got down to it. We would be middle-of-the-road, but make sufficient noises, we hoped, to keep both the right wing and the woollies at bay when the report came out.

Our big breakthrough came in a hotel ballroom in Hull's new dockside marina. We had to define 'attainment targets' for each age and stage from 5-16 which made clear the specific areas of work to be covered and the standards to be achieved. At the same time the total load had to be one with which teachers could reasonably be expected to cope. On the day in question we had a mere 354 attainment targets, all on separate sheets of paper pinned to the walls. Our feet clattered on the dance floor as we circled them to a slow and silent waltz.

Margaret Brown, a lady mathematician from London suddenly shouted 'Eureka!', and suggested a formula for finding the essentials and grouping them together. Within an hour of the breakthrough we had whittled them down to a manageable 14. A few years later at the NCC we got them down to five, but that was child's play by comparison. Needless to say, Kenneth Baker was delighted, and sent us a warm note of congratulation.

Although a close-run thing, the final report was delivered on time, and to everybody's relief was well received by ministers and, to a predictably lesser extent, by teachers. The content was never seriously challenged, and nobody ever accused us of missing out anything vital, or was able to tell us what should be cut out. Since then successive secretaries of state have pared it away, partly to reduce teachers' workload, partly because of that typically British reaction: frightened by unexpected success, we timidly back off. What we have now no longer guarantees that every child will get the essential grounding he or she so urgently needs. The national curriculum, it seems to be forgotten, was devised to prevent schools selling pupils short.Now they're at it again with full ministerial backing. Such is life.

Kenneth Baker was delighted, and said so. Sheer relief may have increased the generosity of his praise. The report largely escaped criticism from the Tory right as it quite obviously preserved standards and 'rigour' (a coded word for the good old days when men were men and calculators hadn't been invented). At each stage we set targets higher than those existing in schools, and stressed the value both of modern methods and good old tables. We managed to hit the middle ground, appealing to both parents and industrialists.

To my pleasant surprise, Humberside was glad to have me back full-time. Perhaps absence had made the heart grow fonder. In reality, mutual trust was developing. Provided the aims of politicians were reputable and above board, my team of officers could deliver them. Terry Geraghty went so far as to say that he'd missed my advice on the days I'd been away in London.

One bit of advice he steadfastly rejected. Humberside was not popular with the natives, who could not identify with it. There were constant demands for its dismemberment, and Humberside signs at roadsides were vandalised and sometimes replaced with beautifully-faked Yorkshire ones. Hull wanted to declare UDI and it now cost 50p more to cross the Humber Bridge. In spite of that, as an administrative unit Humberside worked well, and much new industry was attracted to Hull, Grimsby, and Immingham. My advice to the Council was to change its name to 'East Yorkshire, North Lincolnshire and Hull' — a mouthful, admittedly, but an evocative one. 'Humberside' was soulless, too evidently the end-product of an adman's brief. An informal floating of the new name was well received. We designed new headed notepaper based on a EYNLH logo. Surprisingly, for people usually so sensitive to the public mood, the councillors rejected the idea. As Humberside finally disappeared in 1996, I wondered if it might have survived under a more evocative name. Who knows what's in a name!

CHAPTER NINETEEN

Royal Humberside

IF the royals didn't like the name Humberside, it certainly didn't deter them from coming. To Suffolk they often came privately at weekends. To Humberside they came formally and frequently — 13 trips in my 18 months there. Each one of these was a major event in its own right, requiring a plan drawn up with split-second timing and military precision (and like most battle plans likely to go disastrously wrong). Even the simplest could run to several pages and was the product of summit-meetings involving court staff, myself, the chief constable, and the Lord Lieutenant of the County, Sir Joshua Rowley, not to mention the chairman's flunkeys. The lord lieutenant is the Queen's representative in a county; if he is wise he delegates all the hard work to county officials.

If I look back no more than ten years, I marvel at how attitudes have changed in such a relatively short space of time. There were no open republicans then. Union Jacks did not need to be handed out to tiny crowds to simulate mass enthusiasm. The local populace was there, vociferously and in great numbers, wherever the royals went. Press coverage was massive and comprehensive. Looked at from the inside, as I watched the shameless manipulation by palace staff, I realised how much it was all an illusion, carefully nurtured and dependent on reverence and respect. Even then I marvelled at how fragile the whole edifice was, how vulnerable. Now shattered by scandal and tabloid combined, it can never be rebuilt. Robert Burns (no monarchist himself) caught the imagery well: 'Or like the rainbow's lovely form, vanishing before the storm.'

In the late 1980s I was as captivated as anyone, and though I cursed the workload I felt privileged — it was as if proximity to the Queen or Princess Di made me temporarily exalted too. Familiarity in time bred, if not contempt, disillusion — stripped of the glamour they are just like the rest of us in their needs and attitudes, perhaps a bit narrower even. What really got to me was not that; it was the depths to which some people would go to 'be presented'. Cut-throat ladies in fancy hats and their best costumes and court shoes, parrying each other's umbrella thrusts in the struggle to get close to the Queen, was not a pretty sight — and that was only the committee chairmen's wives. While their men-folk shrunk away, they jostled and pushed — one of the aforementioned managed to be presented twice by dint of ducking down the line and muscling in again six places down from her first handshake! On another occasion it was down the fire-escape, a quick lap round the fire station and in the lower door for a second fleeting embrace. Nothing in 30 years of public life put me under greater pressure than the question of who went where in those wretched presentation lines. Through it all to this day my admiration for the Queen herself remains undiminished. She occasionally would smile wanly at me, as she saw out of the corner of her eye a minor fracas down the line, but her greeting to everyone she met was warm and genuine — up to several hundred times a day!

The fun with a royal visit started literally at the moment of arrival, usually at Humberside International Airport. Precedence between the chairman of the county council and that of the district in which she first set foot, was a grey area. Sometimes we got a deal — if she was just passing through to open, say, a county school, it could be county first, district second scenario. At other times no compromise was possible — my suggestion on one occasion to toss a coin was not well received. Often it meant that even if the Queen was merely hopping from an Andover of the royal flight to a limousine, the mayor of Glanford, complete with chains, would be there with wife, chief executive and half-a-dozen hangers on, simply to shake hands and go home again.

When a royal arrival at the airport was expected, those to be presented arrived in the departure lounge and were placed in order of precedence then marched onto the tarmac. There they were lined up with top guy for the day on the right edge of the red carpet which had been laid out for 50 yards onto the deserted but expectant apron. Some time later the Andover, shining and glisteningly immaculately, would land and taxi round the apron, with the Royal Standard fluttering in the breeze. I never found out how they did that — did it pop out of a recess on top of the cockpit? With uncanny skill the pilot would always park the plane with the steps lining up exactly at the far end of the carpet. Soon the royal personage would emerge in a welter of officials, bodyguards and ladies-in-waiting. If the latter included the Duchess of Grafton then I was sure of a warm greeting. As the royal advanced across the carpet, most but not all of the jostling in the line would cease and presentations begin. Resplendent in a uniform of black, red, and gold, with sword at side and spurs at heel, Sir Joshua would lead the royal visitor down the line. I stood next to the county chairman, and in time came to receive a word of recognition, including once a 'You again' from Di. Then into the limousine which as if by magic appeared on cue at the end of the line and off in a cavalcade of police cars and motor-cycle outriders. For me, normally, a fraught day of trying to keep us to timetable, followed.

Two arrivals stand out from the others. On one occasion as the Queen walked down the carpet, the royal Rolls-Royce, with a couple of Daimlers in tow, appeared and drove straight over the carpet with wet and muddy tyres. As the Rolls pulled up our sovereign and her ladies were left dodging between the Daimlers. The line broke and a mêlée ensued, and the cars tried to move off, adding to the confusion. The Queen coped with glorious dignity and professional poise. The post-mortem revealed that an expansive gesture by the chief constable had been misinterpreted by some wretched minion, who presumably was soon back tramping the beat in downtown Hull as a punishment. How easily ceremony can be reduced to hilarious farce. By the time the Queen had been introduced to what was left of the line, the cars had circled round to the other side of the plane!

I also vividly remember the day that Princess Diana came to open an extension to the airport and to visit a cycle factory in Brough. By now we had reached the point where she would pass me by with just a word and a smile, but on this occasion, after my usual clumsy attempt to bow and shake hands at the same time, she asked me how long the extension had taken to build, and how much it had cost? 'Eighteen months, Ma'am, and a cost of £250,000,' I replied. 'Thank you,' she said. I spent the rest of the visit on tenterhooks hoping she would not ask anyone who knew the real answers to the same questions. If she did, she spared my blushes.

After a tour of the factory, the Princess was presented with tiny bicycles for the infant Princes William and Harry but did not make a speech — she was still in her 'apprentice' stage and did not speak publicly 'off the cuff'. When she rose to leave she stood up 'by numbers' — feet together, a willow of those shapely legs (no cellulite rumours then) and she was up. It was a fascinating insight to set against the maturity and media skill she employed in that later famous *Panorama* interview. Such was her sheer beauty and unsophisticated charm that day that, like most other men, I was hopelessly smitten, and seriously contemplated never washing again the hand she touched in farewell when she'd had to 'do the line' again at the airport late in the day as a final treat before flying off to Dyce and Balmoral.

Engraved for ever in my heart are the events which led up to the opening of the fire station in Hull. At first we were told the Queen was coming by train, disembarking at a small station on the outskirts of Hull. That alone required a top-level site meeting. Gathered together on a windy platform were Sir Joshua, myself, and the stationmaster from York, complete with bowler hat. Nearby the chief constable was squinting through his fingers presumably working out fields of fire for his marksmen. All went well until we discovered that the platform was too short for the royal train! I was vividly reminded of that glorious scene in Charlie Chaplin's *The Great Dictator* when they couldn't get the train to stop at the red carpet where Hitler stood ready to greet Mussolini. Were we going to have to stop a carriage at a time? We walked down the line to where the engine might come to rest, the chief thoroughly alarmed at the security implications. As we wrestled with this seemingly intractable problem a little man, a native of Glasgow, came running down the line to shout: 'Hey mister, she's no gauna come on ra train after a'.' Ah well, back to the apron at

Humberside International, with the chief mentally dismantling the roadblocks and tank traps.

One tank trap remained. The Queen was going to open a 'county' fire station, but it was in Hull! Basil of the ermine robes came to Beverley to tell me that for a thousand years at least, the first thing a reigning monarch did when arriving in Hull was to 'touch the sword'. Apparently this sword was a massive double-handed affair which the mayor of Hull and the chief executive carried between them, proffered to the monarch who touched it as a symbol of something-or-other, after which they retreated and normal life, as we know it, resumed. He insisted this be done at the fire station. In vain did I suggest waiting until Her Majesty got to the town-hall steps where the populace of Hull could witness pomp in all its circumstance. In the end and with some malice, and the connivance of palace officials, it was arranged that they would lurk just inside the railings of the fire station. When she arrived the Queen would step from the Rolls, touch the sword, climb in again and proceed another hundred yards to the archway of firemen with hoses shouldered, waiting to welcome her to their station.

I believe totally in the efficacy of prayer. Not only did it rain, it bucketed. I shall treasure for ever, the two bedraggled figures, ermines sodden and ruined beyond repair, cowering in the downpour. The Queen comfortably beat all records as she got out of the Rolls, touched the sword, and got back in again. She also found time to transfix them with as withering and pitying a look as a Windsor in full flow can muster. Next day I sent Basil back the robes catalogue just in case he had to order a new set.

I still have the brochure which commemorates the royal visit with pictures of the Queen proceeding along the 'line' of guests — a yard apart to cut down the jostling — myself 'hovering' just in case, together with pictures of firemen 'rescuing' the victims of a fire staged in the training tower with ladders, hoses and smoke everywhere. I see that I later congratulated the chief fire officer on the acting skills of his staff, surmising that some might soon find employment in the Royal Shakespeare Company. An equerry, Kenneth Scott, enthused on how much the Queen enjoyed the display and tactfully refrained from mentioning how the smoke canisters somehow got out of control, leading to a royal cough or two, and a change of frock before proceeding to the town hall in Hull for lunch at yet another reception.

I enjoyed the cavalcade of cars on these occasions with motorcycle outriders on either side, all the traffic-lights at green and policemen with white gloves stationed at every intersection. It was also simply fun to charge at full speed through the barriers of the Humber Bridge without paying.

Leaving the fire station, the Queen and the Duke of Edinburgh arrived in Hull in brilliant sunshine and it was gratifying to see that the ermine robes of the Mayor and Basil still looked bedraggled — the phrase 'drowned rats' irresistibly came to mind. After lunch shared with a mere 300 or so, two columns were formed for yet more presentations — one on each side of the banqueting hall. With the perversity which I had come to expect, Prince Philip made for 'hers' rather than 'his', got there before the mayor, recognised me in the background and beckoned me imperiously to do the honours. It wasn't even my show, it was Hull's, we were at the wrong end of the line, and he was in one of his moods. This was no time for explanations or excuses — off we went, and as he spoke to each one, I dashed to the next to try to get some clue as to who they were, in order to introduce them. What an ordeal; we were virtually sprinting down the line. We 'did' ours, crossed the hall, and met the Queen halfway down her line. We won by a line and a half to a half! Only years before in Felixstowe when a grumpy Princess Anne arrived at a Duke of Edinburgh's Award ceremony two hours late, have I seen a faster royal gallop! I must say that, unlike her father, Anne seems to improve with age, and is now extremely popular, not least in Scotland where she supports the right team at Murrayfield. Were an independent Scotland ever given a choice of monarch, I have no doubt that Anne would be 'elected' unanimously.

There was to be one more disaster that day, after the confusion in the banqueting hall. Sir Joshua Rowley, the Lord Lieutenant might kindly have been described as 'endearing'. Amiable, dignified, well-bred he undoubtedly was. An intellectual giant he was not. Briefing him for his part in a royal 'one-engagement day' was no mean task, but on days like this we had to resort by late afternoon to writing cryptic instructions on the back of his immaculate white gloves — like the Princess of Wales, he did it by numbers. Struggling a bit by now, off we went to open a nursery. The Queen and Sir Joshua mounted the dais, the sun pouring down on them, and as he rose to speak, Sir Joshua felt the heat and took off his gloves! Chaos ensued, compounded when an aide rushed to plead with him to put them on again, and as he craned forward to hear her, he caught his sword between his legs, and ended up on his knees. Fortunately, as I had written his programme I was able (shades of Mrs Cowley in Suffolk) to embark on one of those 'I believe that the Lord Lieutenant would have said ...' speeches, while the St John's Ambulance men disentangled him from his sword and spurs, on one of which they found to their evident puzzlement a white glove, with notes 1-5 on the back. Thereafter, following the precedent set by Maitland Mackie when Lord Lieutenant of Aberdeenshire, a policeman was detailed to follow Sir Joshua to 'pick up the pieces'.

At the post-mortem next day in his stately home, we sat in the drawing room, gazing over manicured lawns to the ha-ha and sipped Earl Grey tea, surrounded by the customary untidy welter of papers, gundogs, and back numbers of *Tatler* so typical of the homes of the aristocracy. Silver-framed portraits of the family and of years of royal visits lay in anarchic confusion on the antique bureau and his desk. As we wondered what to do next, a telegram arrived from the Queen, comforting and solicitous, a lovely and revealing touch which cheered up Sir Joshua no end.

Our next engagement was the inauguration of North Sea Ferries' latest super-ferry the *Norsea*, the last big passenger ship to be built on the Clyde (in 1987). At almost 32,000 tons she was a magnificent 'mini-liner' ushering in a new era on the service from Hull to Rotterdam. I was accompanied by my teenage daughter Kirsty who found herself seated for lunch next to Princess Margaret at a large round table in the ship's spacious restaurant. Kirsty was as excited as you could imagine — a real Princess within touching distance. Sad to say, her illusions were shattered. Ignoring her completely Margaret smoked between courses, and even had the odd gasp between bites! To complete the assault on the etiquette Kirsty had properly acquired, Margaret took out her compact and lipstick between dessert and cheese, and gave herself a quick make over. Her off-hand rudeness to the waitresses was a bit of a revelation too. A natural royalist, I was beginning even then to wonder how long all this could go on, and was uncomfortably aware that much, too much perhaps, depended on the Queen herself. Despite his good intentions and obvious desire to succeed, Charles, on the evidence of my own experience, was going to find this a hard act to follow. But in 1987, the magic still worked. After a tour of the bridge and the engine-room, Princess Margaret emerged on the quay to be greeted by thousands of loyal subjects, cheering and waving Union Jacks.

My growing ambivalence about the royal family was fortified four years later in 1991 when an embossed invitation came from the Master of the Household who informed me that he had 'received her Majesty's command to invite Mr Duncan Graham to a Luncheon to be given at Buckingham Palace by the Queen and the Duke of Edinburgh on Wednesday, 1st May, at 12.50 for 1pm. Dress lounge suit.' You can guess that I RSVP'd. Among my fellow guests, ten in number, were a learned judge, a reverend canon, a famous artist, a lady described as 'Director General, British Invisibles', and Will Carling, captain of the English rugby team, and not as yet acquainted with the Princess of Wales.

We met in the 1844 Room, where we were put at ease by members of the household. I spent some of my time trying to do the same for an obviously nervous Will Carling. The poise which comes with practice was in the future for him. We had been advised that each one of us would have an informal chat with both Queen and Consort. At 1.15 the double doors opened and they appeared, together with several assorted corgis — it was a delightful moment.

After introductions, we moved through to lunch. I found that I had been placed on the left of Prince Philip, facing Lord Justice Woolf, and next to the 'invisibles' lady, the Hon. Mrs Wright. I discovered the hard way that according to convention the royals converse exclusively with the guest on their right until vegetables are served with the main course. Then the guest on the left gets the 'full undivideds.' At first I thought that the prince was simply ignoring me as he spoke to Lady Littler, a television VIP. Meanwhile, I learned from Mrs Wright that 'invisibles' were exports you could not see! I also learned, by watching like a hawk, what the protocol of service was — elegantly-attired waiters proffered salvers from which one helped oneself — no French service. Sitting next to a duke inhibits the appetite, so I nibbled at the cornets de salmon fumé en crabe, and sipped abstemiously of the Kreuznacker Brüches Spätlese 1985, while marvelling at the beauty of the porcelain, the cutlery and the cruets.

The main course was poussin, poéle mascotte, with a multitude of vegetables and salads on which to choke, or to spill from the salvers. I was only just coping with these potential booby traps when I found I had the prince to myself. It turned out to be something of a mixed blessing. He didn't think much of the national curriculum, of which I was in charge, and was inclined to ascribe the ills of the nation to a lack of team games on the playing fields of comprehensive schools. He knew nothing of recent changes in education, and cared even less. Short of provoking a punch-up, there was little I could do, and it was with great relief that after agreeing to differ we dispatched our marquise au chocolat, washed down with Royal Vintage 1955. It was a wonderful, unforgettable experience, but the gulf between real life and the duke's perceptions of it seemed unbridgeable. Distressingly, he showed little inclination to learn.

Coffee was served in an adjoining room, and I was privileged to enjoy a quarter of an hour or so sitting with the Queen on a chaise longue, with a corgi at our feet. In addition to that magic 'something', which I had experienced before at my investiture, she displayed warmth, interest, a surprising knowledge, and a quiet unexpected humour. You would not expect me to reveal the contents of a royal aside relating to another lady elected, rather than born, to office. It is not always easy to identify the high points of one's life, but for me, this was and will remain one of them.

Looking back with the benefit of hindsight and with the Queen now a septuagenarian, it is easy to see how much the place of royalty depends on that grand illusion. Shatter it and nothing on earth can rebuild it. We will never again see the pitch of excitement, the anticipation that gripped Humberside, as elsewhere, on a royal visit in the 1980s. No longer do thousands turn up unprompted, hours before the great event. Lord lieutenants strut still, chief constables no doubt worry about security, chief executives inevitably fret over detail, but something beyond price has gone. The modest monarchy of the future will surely move less ostentatiously through the land, and the programmes of royal days will no longer run to seven pages, double-column.

CHAPTER TWENTY

The March to York

IN May 1987, with the Mathematics Working Party barely two months from presenting its report, and with some of its members in Japan trying to find out how Japanese children were so much ahead of ours in numeracy, I made my way with sinking heart to the monthly confrontation which passed for the full all-day (and night) meeting of council. Far from rubber-stamping the decisions of a dozen service committees, virtually every issue was debated afresh and at length, usually in the vain hope of a headline in the local rag. I had taken to concealing a paperback in my papers, to while away the hours. It was worth the risk of being drawn in without having listened to the arguments — after all, nobody else had. A note was passed to me as I sat on the dais beside the chairman. Would I phone the secretary of state's private secretary asap? Later in the day I found the note which I had forgotten about, in the pages of the Patrick O'Brian novel I had been reading. The official was a bit miffed at my tardy response and said Kenneth Baker wished me to join him for lunch next day. I declined on the grounds that council might well last another day. In any case I had had enough of governments and national curricula.

'This is extremely urgent,' he said. I remained unmoved. He phoned back: 'How about the next evening?' My curiosity was aroused, and I had come to like Baker personally. I boarded the train at York at teatime and in due course made my way by the tube to

Elizabeth House. I was ushered into the famous waiting-room with portraits of Baker's 21 predecessors since the second world war, starting with Ellen Wilkinson and including Margaret Thatcher, the only one of them to go on to be prime minister. Idly I worked out that on average they had all lasted a fraction over a year in office, a statistic which explains the extreme urgency of politicians to make their mark. It has to be quickly or not at all.

Into the room came the ebullient Jenny Bacon, a senior civil servant not out of the usual mould. She cycled to the DES daily and parked her bike in her office with the front wheel in the waste-paper basket. The only occasion on which she had been sighted in a skirt had been the day she was summoned to explain policy to the Archbishop of Canterbury. Public school and Oxbridge, she had infiltrated the Whitehall establishment but was not truly 'one of them' any more than I was. She broke it to me that Baker had combined the posts of chairman and chief executive of the about-to-be-formed NCC, and intended to offer me the job. Mind awhirl, I was whisked into the secretary of state's inner sanctum to find Baker smiling from ear to ear. He greeted me like an old friend, poured me a generous dram of an excellent malt before anything was said. We sat down in the armchairs reserved for VIPs.

He then offered me what he called 'the most important job in education and certainly one of the most influential'. I was a 'can do' man and that was unusual among educationists, he said flatteringly. As we talked, replenishing our glasses, his personal dedication to the task ahead shone through the shell of cynicism which politicians all too often hide behind. Standards and quality existed in the best schools, but not uniformly elsewhere. Every child deserved the best. His enthusiasm, commitment and his interest in equal opportunities was remarkable in a Tory minister and tied in closely with my own ideals, formed in the Gorbals and Finnieston so many years before. In a world where I had come to question the motives of most of those involved in the education racket, his approach was all the more refreshing. I was to discover it was genuine, even if not shared by his cabinet colleagues, and definitely not by the prime minister. I was aware that other vested interests in Whitehall might not go along with him. I should have remembered how transient the life of an education secretary is, and perhaps speculated more than I did on who might succeed him.

The NCC would have a membership of 15 chosen by Baker, and would be a quango (quasi-autonomous non-governmental organisation) entrusted with putting the flesh on the bones of the 1988 Education Act, turning the reports of the ten subject working parties, starting with my own mathematics one, into a reality which could be taught in schools. There was an ambassadorial role 'selling' the new way at home and abroad — not the least to teachers, who were rightly sceptical. The appointment would not be a political one — I would not be expected to toe the party line.

As we sat there, my mind was working in overdrive. From what I knew of the proposed revolution — and that's what it was — it was going to be a close-run thing between an ambitious, over-elaborate but fundamentally sound attempt to bring about genuine improvement, and a right-wing hijack, as my mathematics experience with Sig Prais had demonstrated. Baker did not refer directly to that. He was having problems and I knew this only too well, but we did not talk about them openly. We understood each other. I had to balance the risks, and the consequences of leaving Humberside with so much still to do, against the excitement, and a sense of duty. I have always argued if you can't beat 'em, join 'em. I knew the dangers of the whole thing getting out of control if someone did not get a grip of it, and I believed that I had some chance of doing so, behind the scenes. Deep down, I was amused at this key English initiative being offered to a Scot with little sympathy for extreme right views and a lifelong concern for fairness and equality. How had I avoided being blackballed — my opposition to cuts and selection were public knowledge?

There was a silence and I realised that both Baker and his permanent secretary were looking at me, awaiting a response. It was an irresistible challenge. I said yes — on one condition. The headquarters of the new body could not be in London. It was agreed that I could choose the location, provided it was treasury-approved. What I did not know then was that the geographical outer limit of civil service thinking was Milton Keynes — after that you fall off the end of the world. I was thinking of York: a fine city within reach of home, and only two hours from London by InterCity 125. I was often in central

London faster than folks from the outskirts of the city. Instinctively too, I wanted breathing space away from the Whitehall hothouse. Later it was to be argued that our problems may have stemmed from being too far away from the centre of things. On balance I think that we gained more than we lost. The 'Whitehall Village' is pretty remote from the rest of us, inward-looking and incestuous. As I write a BBC news report on a bomb incident in London quotes Scotland Yard as saying 'The bomb was on the far side of Hammersmith Bridge.' Far from whom? In similar vein I came to feel that it must be literally uphill from London to York. I was expected to get to London in good time for 9am meetings while those in York could never commence before 11am. By half-past two in the afternoon Londoners were visibly fretting to be away. Perhaps the last train to civilisation left at 4pm?

Later, I was to find that even York was too close for comfort, especially at weekends. Most politicians are quite incapable of switching off from their introverted world be it Whitehall or Islington, which makes them liable to pick up the phone at any hour of the day or night. The patrician Douglas Hurd has publicly lamented this trait in his colleagues, which hardly helps them to maintain a healthy sense of proportion. The last straw was a call at midnight on Saturday from a cabinet minister to let me know that he and some friends had come up with a super wheeze at a dinner party which he would like me to work up for a meeting on Monday morning. The outcome was that I purchased a weekend flat in Appleby and had the phone taken out.

In the train back that night I had time to set my excitement against the enormity of what faced me. Nationwide consultations on mathematics and science were due in August, and, with neither staff nor base, I would not be free of Humberside until September. In spite of the frustrations, I have never regretted the fateful decision made that night. I'm not sure if anyone in Humberside regretted it, but I like to think that some did.

We opened for business in July 1988 — without a brass plate — in a disused office above an insurance office in the centre of York. There were four of us, my deputy Peter Watkins, and two office staff. There were five telephones, all in separate rooms, and we had to sprint madly about whenever one of them phone rang. It was symbolic of the future — we usually got to things just when other people had rung off. I had no job specification and no budget. The former was helpful in terms of getting things done, the latter the start of a battle with hard-nosed civil servants who resorted to shameless bribery — do it our way if you want cash and staff.

Finding a new permanent headquarters for the 70 staff it was finally agreed we could have, posed an unexpected problem. We chose an 'off-the-peg' job being put up by a contractor on the site of the old Queen's Hotel, close to the river, which was due to be completed in less than a year. The archaeologists, who have in York the right to dig in every site before it disappears forever under tons of concrete, suddenly came across what they claimed to be fragments of the palace of the Roman Emperor Septimus Severus, a find of priceless significance. I could not believe it. I was full of sympathy in one sense, distraught and potentially homeless in another. This could go on for years!

We were soon at the epicentre of a storm of protest. Preservationists led by Richard Hall the archaeologist escalated the significance of the find — it was a test case for them to have ad lib access to sites in York. On the other hand the city fathers feared not only that we would have to leave York for rival Doncaster, but also that no other prestigious bodies would risk coming to York. Eight other sites were simultaneously frozen from development. After a lot of arm-twisting behind the scenes a deal was struck: government cash to speed up excavation work, and permission to go ahead for us. Then real disaster struck. The local Tory MP, with the smallest majority in England, decided to make a name for himself by 'saving the site for the nation'. To my surprise, he evidently decided there were more votes in Roman remains than in jobs. Off he dashed to the Environment Secretary, Nicholas Ridley, who slapped a preservation order on the site. The archaeologists showed at least as much consternation as I did. A full investigation might reveal that they had over-egged their claims. Septimus Severus must have been creasing himself in his crypt. I certainly wasn't!

In the end another site was found for us on Albion Wharf, right on the river. The views would be magnificent, even if there was a risk of flooding whenever the Ouse was in spate. Of course, the archaeologists could have held this up too, but now we knew their secrets. They wisely ruled that as the site had been in the bed of the river in mediaeval times there would be no significant remains! The contractors dug up plenty of intriguing relics, including the tail bones of several hundred oxen in one heap. It was all quickly obliterated in ready-mix concrete six-feet deep — who knows what might have been. Jobs versus conservation is a topic I now avoid.

Robert Pilcher, the builder, had mainly built houses before and Albion Wharf was his chance to gain a name for himself. He built his monument with loving care, far beyond specification, with marbled walls and terrazzo tiling — all at his own expense, as we would simply rent on a 25-year lease. In a time of austerity, this did our image no good at all: the papers were full of stories of collapsing primary schools with outside toilets which could be refurbished for a fraction of what we were spending! In vain did I try to set the record straight — the hares were already running.

The story of the Albion Wharf carpet as I have already mentioned was more of the same, and has dogged my steps ever since. I was too busy other than to show a distant interest when Robert Pilcher and an architect suggested that on the third floor, where the committee chamber was, the carpet should have a pattern bearing the NCC logo. How I wish I'd paid more attention. Soon the rumours spread that it had cost an extraordinary price per square yard, and at my personal behest vast sums of money had been expended. What profligate and wanton waste ... the tabloids wanted to hear of nothing else. Condemnation wrestled with righteous indignation. I had been well and truly carpeted! In fact the carpet had cost no more than the run-of-the-mill covering of the other floors, the cost had been borne by the builder and our rent was unaffected. No one wanted to hear — we even came close to being the subject of questions in the House of Commons. When the NCC moved out years later, bits of the carpet were kept as souvenirs which was a more permanent epitaph for the carpet than for the NCC. I'm still questioned about it today when I address education groups. I haven't got a piece and ironically regarded it as rather vulgar from the start.

When I think of the building, now the home of the Schools Funding Council for grant-maintained schools, I recall it most vividly for the floods. After heavy rain, the water from about a quarter of England funnels through York — and quite a sight it is. It was calculated that it would flood the car park twice a year on average, and might reach the floor above once a century. So much for statistics. Within six months we had it lapping at the entrance three times, and once it flooded the street outside, literally marooning those inside as a menacing brown tide whirled past at three knots. Thirty feet away folks stood outside the pub watching us, supping their ale in total normality. The flood stopped an inch below the main electricity supply board and we lost only the lift mechanism, thoughtfully installed in the basement. As a fisherman I had in my office a pair of thigh-waders. I braved the swirling waters, reached terra firma with the first of our lady staff on my back. The rest refused to risk it. Rather understandably the emergency services were busy elsewhere, so I made my way to the nearest yacht chandlers where I purchased a 9ft Avon rubber dinghy. We inflated it beside the pub and rowed the rest of the staff to safety. Just as well my job specification was so all-embracing.

I hope that the funding council have looked after the dinghy well. It was certainly a talking point for visitors on calm summer days. From my window I normally looked down on the bridge of a sand dredger moored at the quay. On that day I exchanged greetings with the skipper literally eye to eye. He could have stepped into my room had he been so minded. Beset by natural disasters, we could well have done without the storms already brewing in London. A query from the Audit Office as to why we'd invested in a boat was the least of my worries.

PART V

Whitehall and York

CHAPTER TWENTY-ONE

The Curriculum Racket

Any doubts which I had that the main players in the education game had the remotest interest in children, classrooms and teachers were dispelled in the next three years. There were far more important issues than the future of the nation. Those with a masochistic desire for a blow-by-blow account may read the book I wrote with David Tytler in 1993, *A Lesson For Us All — the making of the National Curriculum*. Here it will suffice to reflect on the highs, and more frequently, the lows. There is much to ponder.

Although by this time, after 20 years' experience of local and national government, I was accustomed to hidden agendas, empire building, vested interests and sheer self-interest, what was now to unfold surprised me both by its scale and audacity. Sometimes actions could be excused by fear and insecurity, more often there were no redeeming features.

I had imagined that as an administrative offshoot of the DES as it then was, 'they' would be broadly speaking, on my side. What a mistake that was. The arcane rulebook by which civil servants work identifies quangos as the enemy and defines them, at best, as being both troublesome and wayward. When one of them threatens the Whitehall power base it becomes dangerous. The NCC by its very nature did just that. The DES, often accused by other departments of weakness because it had to work with and through LEAs, had after a hundred years of trying finally got its hands on the curriculum and it wasn't going to let go easily to an upstart in York. Kenneth Baker's aside a few months later that the NCC had been set up to keep the mandarins in check was a delicious irony. From the start senior civil servants exerted legitimate pressure, as they saw it, by swamping our meetings. They could outnumber us as we deliberated, encamped in a menacing outer ring, making us feel like pioneers in a wagon train at night, and demand to see every document in draft. Less legitimate and more insidious means included holding up everything, questioning every penny of expenditure, paring back on staff. They had more financial wizards watching us than we had to run our own affairs! They had developed into an art form the line that they 'spoke for the minister and with his approval'. By preventing my meeting him as far as possible, they made it difficult to verify this.

Minister's private secretaries are junior civil servants, frequently ambitious enough to feel it necessary to eavesdrop on ministers' phonecalls, and sift through their letters, tipping off their seniors about 'unauthorised' approaches by quango bosses. It was fun to an extent dropping them false clues, but in reality it was too serious a game for that. By the time John McGregor was Secretary of State for Education, he and I phoned in the evenings to our homes if we wanted a private chat. I scarcely ever managed to meet with Baker, McGregor or Clarke in the DES without a clutch of civil servants present, not to mention HMI. They tried to stage manage meetings by 'briefing' innocents like me beforehand, helpfully telling one what 'the minister would like to hear'. It was all very exhausting and frustrating. Real schools and real pupils staggered under a weight of conflicting advice while the power game was played behind closed doors.

Democracy was not a concept with which the mandarins found themselves at ease. When, as chairman, I allowed members of council to range widely over a topic, often thinking the unthinkable before drawing a debate to a practical conclusion, I was frequently interrupted by a deputy permanent secretary lecturing us on the need to confine ourselves only to what ministers 'expected'. A few hours in the council chamber in Beverley or Paisley would have done him no end of good. The art of democracy is not to stifle debate, but to get the required outcome, with everyone feeling that they have had their say.

I watched the mandarins shamelessly perform all the tricks so gloriously exposed in *Yes, Minister* — bland non-committal assurances, delaying tactics, ridicule, and if all else failed, a committee to 'investigate' at length. Before my very eyes the DES set up a committee composed entirely of MPs, civil servants, LEA chairmen and industrialists, to oversee the in-service training of teachers, without a single teacher or education administrator on it. The long-awaited results were entirely predictable; by then most of us had forgotten the committee's purpose.

It was not long before I and my colleagues were being regarded as 'troublemakers'. Without the requisite public school/Oxbridge background perhaps, I was felt to be 'unsound'. I treasure the day I was taken aside and told I had the wrong end of a very important stick. 'Look here, old son, don't get emotionally involved. You care too much and it's clouding your overall grasp of what all this is about.'

I pled guilty but was unrepentant. I was visiting schools every week where the grand design was, to put it mildly, faltering. I was to grow accustomed to this yawning gulf between the perceptions of politicians and reality. When I pointed this out, right-wing politicians tended to class me as a 'dangerous leftie' and once even a 'Marxist'. Left-wing teacher agitators accused me of being a right-wing lackey. Not bad going for a lifelong floating voter. Like so many others who took a different view from the Tory right on any topic, I was to learn that I was being 'unhelpful' if not downright obstructive.

The DES was engaged in a naked power bid and was willing to harness right-wing political views if it helped their cause. With no experience of running a sweety shop, never mind a school, they relied on compliant enthusiasts and committed extremists, tempering their views less and less with the advice of professionals, which they found increasingly tiresome.

For a fatally long period, Her Majesty's Inspectors, led by a man of great ability and total integrity, Eric Bolton, kept their distance from the NCC. To an extent this was understandable as they had had the curriculum pretty well to themselves for generations and rightly prized their right to speak fearlessly and with authority. Now they had to deal with not one, but two usurpers: DES and, as they saw it, NCC. In the early days they held rival meetings to NCC ones on the new curriculum, saying different things, denigrating us in public, and causing hopeless confusion in an area already obscure in the extreme. No wonder conscientious teachers despaired and had nervous break-downs, torn between awed respect for HMI and statutory legally-binding advice from NCC. What I did not appreciate then was that HMI were themselves under great threat. Their balanced, informed approach was anathema to the right wing of the Tory party; embar-rassing too, when they exposed the squalor of school buildings and the painful lack of money to introduce a new curriculum which entailed the replacement of virtually every text book in the land. In time HMI came to identify their real enemy — the DES were exploiting the inspectors' unpopularity with the right to get them under control. The mandarins may have been jealous of HMI's right to speak their minds based on evidence painstakingly collected in schools.

By that time, however, the horse had bolted, and our belated alliance could no more than slow down the gallop to the right and to impracticality. There were demands to abolish HMI, or to 'privatise' them. How would Her Majesty have felt about a 'Group 4' approach to the education of her subjects? Their fate was grisly — now they are called Ofsted (Office for standards in education), decimated in num-bers, and, with a chief executive widely perceived as a political pawn, his integrity questioned openly by a Tory select committee chairman. The impartial image has been badly dented. HMI's trademark, the measured objective pronouncement, has been replaced by the politi-cally adjusted polemic to the great loss of all.

The national curriculum had to be tested. Ministers and civil ser-vants shared a palpable distrust of teachers — they had, after all, 'gotten us into this fine mess'. A twin to the NCC, the Schools Examination and Assessment Council (SEAC) was set up, in a grim tower block in Notting Hill Gate, to oversee not just GCSE and 'A' level examinations, but a complex barrage of tests to enforce the national curriculum on the lines of 'if it moves, test it to destruction'. The debate which ensued need not concern us in detail here, as the usual clash between the 'high stools and quill pen'-brigade, and the 'test by enjoyment'-school took place. Suffice it to say that teachers were compelled to spend far more time weighing the pig than feeding it — hours and hours testing and marking, scarcely any time left for teaching. Although SEAC's first chairman Philip Halsey, a former civil servant ironically, fought a valiant battle against the odds, the whole thing became a grim farce. Soon what children were taught was being divided into what could be tested and what could not. Unfortunately, most of what really matters — breadth, balance, judgement, the aesthetic and the imaginative — cannot be, by its very nature, easily tested. Dull facts can, and so the richness was gradually squeezed out to the detriment of pupils and society alike. Of course many important things can be tested — spelling, grammar, tables, long division — but these are not the be-all and end-all of life. In order to satisfy its masters SEAC slid down the slippery slope to putting examinability before education, and to achieve that abandoned any pretence that what you teach children is more important than what you test them on. We now have a test-led curriculum. The hoops through which children are forced to pass from the age of five are considered far more important than what passes through them. There is now a well-paid growth industry examining more and more of less and less of what life and education are all about.

When all this was happening, former key players in the education game were either ignored or subjected to the mushroom approach. Every now and then the hatch opened and a load of something unpleasant was shovelled on top of them. Most obvious of these were the teachers expected to implement the new curriculum. It may be true that teachers had lost some credibility in the 1980s, blamed for the excesses of the woolly liberals, and having shot themselves in the foot with strikes, wrangles, and an ill-judged and petty-looking refusal to supervise school meals. In truth they were the victims of a society losing faith in itself. The collapse in standards and the lack of discipline were there in the nation if not its schools. The increase in broken marriages did as much harm or more than the trendiest of teaching. Schools reflect society, they do not shape it.

The national curriculum was a deliberate attempt to put teachers in their place. They were consulted neither about its shaping nor its content. It could be argued that the good that came of it, and there was much, would not have been achieved with the old traditional approach of co-operation and consultation, but the legacy of teacher exclusion was bitterness and hostility. I took on the job at the NCC on the clear understanding that the partnerships would be restored in the implementation phase. I set up subject committees of teachers, involved teaching unions at every stage, and tramped the country talking to and listening at countless meetings. Soon I became aware that I was alone in this. A hostile council increasingly composed of political appointees abolished the committees in a stroke, and treated union leaders with disdain.

An honourable exception who survived the 'packing' of the council was Daphne Gould, head of an inner-city girls' school in London. An ample lady, whose jovial features were precariously topped by a severe 1960's bouffant hairdo (à la Marie Wilson) which was gravitationally challenged, Daphne presided over a magic school. Hardly any of her pupils had English as a first language, many came from cultures in which the place of girls was lowly, but to unbelievable academic success they added poise and self-respect which was a joy to behold. Her curriculum had much more than just ten subjects. Daphne and her staff practised what they preached, took on all comers, and showed what can be achieved if the will is there.

Daphne's was the only head's study I ever visited which contained a fridge, a cooker and a microwave. The vast cake served with elevenses and baked by her own fair hand was cut into real man-size wedges. For lunch she conjured up steaks the size of frying pans, and two soup tureens of chips plus all the trimmings. When I had the tenacity to ask who was joining us for this gargantuan repast, she responded with evident surprise that there was barely enough for two! With a few more Daphnes, the NCC might well have achieved greater things for more children — hers in every way was vision on the grand scale.

Junior ministers such as Tim Eggar and Michael Fallon (his defeat at the polls was for me a little highlight of the 1992 elections) made it abundantly clear what they thought of teachers such as Daphne and those contaminated by association with them. As I visited schools I constantly pondered on the douce middle-of-the-road folk I met, and the raving lefties that politicians seemed able to spot in even the smallest rural primary school. Politicians certainly prefer prejudice to reality. No wonder they keep confusing presentation with substance. Perhaps that is why there is such a high mortality rate among Tory messengers!

We experienced the kind of pressure more familiar in a totalitarian state and were reduced to dropping asides to teachers' leaders, planting questions, and as Professor Michael Barber, then an NUT leader, has revealed in his book, my staff, unbeknown to me, grew adept at slipping copies of 'secret' documents on English to teachers in the NCC's subterranean car-park — presumably when it was not 8ft deep in the turgid waters of the Ouse. In the end trying to square the circle of conscience and duty was to influence my decision to part company with the NCC. Professional integrity was and is far more important to me than using my reputation to sell half-truths, lies and dogma to teaching colleagues. To their great credit teachers in subject groups, and through their leaders, gave the NCC great support. All I can say now is that without them, the end-product would have been significantly worse than it turned out to be. Their dignified frustration at the mishandling of what could have been the salvation of education in England reflects great credit on the noblest, if not the oldest of the professions.

Before devoting a chapter to the politicians — I suppose they deserve one to themselves — it is worth mentioning the other bodies subject to the mushroom approach: the LEAs. The way things went demonstrates the extreme contrast between relationships in the 1960s, 70s and 80s and the present decade. By cut and attack, by legislative diminution of their powers, LEAs have been banished to the periphery of the education scene. They still possessed an organisation which might have pulled off the implementation of the whole vast enterprise. They had advisers, day-to-day links with schools, and whole rafts of expertise. They were calculatedly bypassed. As a result convoys of articulated lorries blocked city-centre and village streets as the DES sought to deal directly with 25,000 schools whose needs they could not even start to understand. No wonder that on the first day of the first national test of seven-year-olds, half the schools didn't have the papers, some of the rest had thrown them out as junk mail, and a few were busily coaching their pupils in advance. If ever there was a lesson that national direction is a recipe for disaster, this was it. Schools which became grant-maintained early on soon found this out the hard way — not much future in phoning Elizabeth House (now moved, would you believe, to Sanctuary Buildings!) for assistance when the pipes burst or the gym burnt down.

By accident or design the views and experience of those who could have increased the chances of success lay neglected. Professional advice was all too often seen as mere obstruction — if you're in a hurry to change the world you don't want to be told that the postal system cannot cope or that teachers are human beings too. In spite of the best efforts of more moderate politicians, the right-wing poured into the void created by bypassing teachers and LEAs. You must form your own judgements as to whether they knew best — better than parents, teachers, industrialists and public. Whose children did they really care about? Most of theirs were tucked away in the independent schools, which were judged so perfect as not to be in need of a national curriculum!

CHAPTER TWENTY-TWO

It Hurts When I Laugh

AT odd moments I had a fleeting sympathy for ministers as they sat atop a seething mass of intrigue, trying to cope with their civil servants, HMI and quangos. At the same time they were coming under increasing pressure from the right wing of their own party. By the mid-1990s the right was to run riot over the issue of Europe and push the party strongly its way. In the times of which we speak, they were fewer in number and the tactics seemed to be to keep them at bay by throwing them occasional buns — the chief of which seemed to be education. Their impact for good or evil was profound and yet individually they were unimpressive — a few zealots from Margaret Thatcher's think-tank and Sheila Lawlor, best known for her relentless attack on teacher training. Here, as elsewhere, there had been legitimate cause for concern, as any teacher who was trained in the 1960s and 70s could acknowledge. But by now the old lags who had patently never faced a class had been weeded out of colleges and universities and training was centred on how to teach rather than arcane theory and the profundities of Pestalozzi and Montessori. As is so often the case the right was shooting behind the target. Sheila Lawlor shared a platform with me on one occasion, addressing the blue-rinsed ladies of the Tory shires in Central Hall, Westminster. I was sure that I was on a hiding to nothing until one lady asked Lawlor how many colleges she had visited to see for herself. 'None' she replied. 'It was not necessary to visit, I just know!'

She got the raspberry she deserved. Next day, the Tory tabloids reported that she had launched a scathing and well-directed attack on lefties in training colleges. That's how myths become fact.

Kenneth Baker stood the pressures well as far as I could see. He regarded the 1988 Education Act as at least the equal of the great Butler Act of 1944 which had paved the way for postwar education. The national curriculum was to be 'as good as the best minds in the country can make it. Content ... should reflect the best practice of our good schools.' He went on 'we can no longer leave individual teachers, schools, or local authorities to decide the curriculum children should follow. It is no longer acceptable that many children have a much less good curriculum than others through the accident of where they happen to go to school.' So far so good. There was even here a hint of equality of opportunity — an entitlement for each child. Would that his successors had taken this to heart. There is now less equality, more stark contrasts than at any time since the war. Hard cheese if you happen to be a pupil in an under-funded, under-performing inner-city school in the mid-1990s.

Baker also announced that there would be ten subjects in the new curriculum. I've often thought that they were precisely those Baker had studied at his prep school — no room for, say, home economics or dance. Pre-eminent were English, maths and science with, in addition, a laudable ambition to have every child study a modern language, as well as history, geography, art, music, PE and 'technology'. We were never clear what this last one was. It sounded good and no doubt originated in Baker's past role as a whizz-kid computer minister. A working group under Lady Parkes, a prominent governor of the BBC, tried valiantly to put flesh on the bones, but even now no one is quite sure what it's all about.

The preamble to the Act of 1988 was equally reassuring. The aim was to: a) promote the spiritual, moral, cultural, mental and physical developments of pupils at the school and of society; and b) prepare such pupils for the opportunities, responsibilities and experiences of adult life.

That's a broad liberal definition to which Baker personally subscribed. The onslaught on it came on two fronts and was led by the prime minister herself. Even ten traditional subjects was too much for the right to stomach — it was more than the 'basics', whatever they were. The next thrust was to make sure that every subject was loaded with facts and knowledge, supported by traditional teaching methods, which meant serried ranks of children facing a teacher, spouting forth; none of this group and individual study nonsense. A striking example of Thatcher's single-minded determination was passed on to me by a civil servant. Apparently in the morning after a great world crisis she was found sitting alone at breakfast altering the wording of the detailed proposals for English, while munching at her toast and marmalade. You might find that magnificent, frightening, or both.

English was to become a major battlefield. Like mathematics the arguments had polarised. The debate centred on the teaching of grammar, the books that children should read, and the importance of reading, writing and spelling. The English working group was headed by Brian Cox, seen as a right-wing trusty. In the1980s he had been behind the extreme 'Black Papers on Education'. He would, it was assumed, give short shrift to the prevailing view that Shakespeare, Wordsworth and Dickens should be dropped, and that correcting mistakes in spelling or punctuation inhibited children in their creative writing (the in-phrase for 'composition'). A recent report had gone so far as to say that children's enjoyment of learning should not be spoiled by worrying about details such as verbs, nouns, pronouns and sentences. As usual the innovators had gone too far. Parsing and analysis can be pretty deadly, but the answer seems to me to lie in better teaching rather than in simply abandoning them. What other country has ever suggested the dropping of its own language's grammar by schools!

To everyone's surprise, from Thatcher's to mine, Cox's interim report distinctly downplayed grammar — 'only one part of the study of language ... taught in context and for a purpose ... likely to arise from problems which pupils have discovered for themselves ... pupils should not do labelling exercises ... not sensible to propose a list of definitive terms.' Cox had, against all the odds, gone native.

His group produced an ill-advised primary book list which arbitrarily cut out Enid Blyton — *Just William* was OK, but not The

Famous Five. Beatrix Potter rubbed shoulders with Oscar Wilde and Spike Milligan in the approved list. Where would it all end? Was it simply advisory or, shades of 1984, would children in time only read what the government laid down? As my own children had read Enid Blyton avidly and despite that handicap gone on to high grades in 'A' level English, I wondered what the harm was.

The NCC backed Baker's view that the group had got the balance wrong, while quietly amused that it had been too far to the left. A revised report was called for to go before my council. Two days before we met, the civil servants' view was that it was now acceptable. A day later Jenny Bacon phoned at 4.30pm to say it was 'totally unaccept-able' and our meeting should be cancelled 'on the instruction of min-isters'. I asked her to spell out to me the four or five things most wrong with it and she fell unwontedly silent. We went ahead. Apparently the lefties on Cox's group had threatened to resign if they did not get their way. They didn't, any more than did my own English officer who turned out to be in sympathy with them. For the one and only time while at the NCC, I had more sympathy with the right. They never forgave Cox and I suspect that Kenneth Baker's card may have been marked for letting it all happen.

Baker was scrupulous in his approach to ministerial involvement in detail. Unlike his successors he did not try to force his own ideas on the curriculum, although he was no doubt tempted as a writer and author himself. He diffidently suggested at one of our rare meetings that it would be nice to see some recitation written in somewhere, quoting at length passages from Keats and Shelley he had learned at school. Who could resist such an approach? It was hardly prejudice and most folks will admit that all they can quote in adulthood is what they had to learn by heart at school. Still, ministerial whim had been enshrined in law — the very thin end of a very thick wedge.

English was a close-run thing; much more dramatic was the battle for what came to be called the 'Whole Curriculum'. To the right, ten subjects were about seven too many. They had no truck with the idea that the whole is more than the sum of the parts. They saw as dan-gerous such topics as the environment, citizenship, economic aware-ness, and moral education. This was, in their view, where left-wing teachers had led youngsters astray. I suspect that if they could themselves have written the script for these subjects they would have been more willing to contemplate them. As it was they saw them only as a needless distraction from the three 'R's. The trouble was that my council, not as yet largely infiltrated by political nominees, thought differently, as did most teachers, parents and, significantly, industrialists, including the CBI. They wanted future employees who were imaginative, could think for themselves, work with other people, and think laterally.

Perhaps rattled by his experiences with English, Baker listened uncritically to his civil servants, who plainly saw the NCC's plans to produce guidance in this area as an unwelcome amendment to their precious blueprint, non-contentious as it seemed and compatible as it was with the ten subjects. And so the roof fell in. A posse of civil servants descended on York (but not before the 11.30 train arrived from London!). All work outside the ten subjects was to stop. The draft guidelines on the entire curriculum were to be suppressed, stillborn. Minor mandarins shook with righteous indignation at our treachery. They produced a two-page letter signed by Baker halting everything but the ten subjects. In a blatant attempt by the civil servants who'd drafted it to get us once and for all, it continued by saying that no papers should ever again be considered, let alone debated, at formal meetings of the council unless 'seen and approved in advance by the Secretary of State'. This was sensational — an allegedly independent body whose work had to be approved even before being discussed and passed on to the minister! In the hands of the press and the Labour Party this would be dynamite. Colleagues advocated 'leaking it' straight away as a prelude to mass resignation.

I had a gut feeling that Baker might just have signed this letter in a pile of others from his red box without fully appreciating its significance. I knew that leading industrialists whom he trusted were on our side. I telephoned him at home, and was well-received. I broke it to him as to what it was that he had signed and he showed great surprise, to put it mildly. His comments on civil servants were unprintable. He speculated on why we seldom met, and concluded that the mandarins had thrown a cordon sanitaire round him. We must meet, but out of sight of the DES mandarins. Pure theatre followed. He suggested a clandestine meeting in Betws-y-Coed in North Wales, where he was going to do a half-marathon for charity. I was in Wales for a conference at the time so we both had perfect cover.

A helicopter was waiting for Baker in the field behind the hotel. Dressed in his running gear, a sight alone which I shall treasure for ever — just the knees for the kilt — he emerged alone, shook me warmly by the hand, and invited me in for coffee. I showed him the letter. He could not believe that he had signed it, or been allowed to sign it. It was a magic moment and a revealing one. The pressures on him were enormous and those who 'served' him were apparently manipulating him. Ruefully we reflected on the remoteness of all this from schools and education.

He accepted that the council could well deliver both ten subjects and some broader advice and the day was saved. The letter was not withdrawn, merely locked safely away (my original had somehow 'disappeared' when I went through my files on leaving). As we walked out to the helicopter, he was visibly shaken and angry. We agreed to meet more often if more orthodoxly. We shook hands, he climbed into the helicopter and was whisked off to the start of his half-marathon. Thus was the breadth of education in England in the 1990s rescued in Betws-y-Coed on a fine June morning.

It was still difficult for us to meet. A frontal approach to Baker's office would ring a thousand alarm bells, and lead to frantic attempts to forestall a meeting. It was gratifying to feel so dangerous — a teacher at large in the beargarden. After some meetings had been blocked, in frustration I approached Sir David Hancock the permanent secretary. We had a delightful lunch at the Athenaeum, the quintessential London club. Over coffee I told him what it was like out there in York. He was too discreet to criticise colleagues, but the dogs of war backed off. It was not before time.

I almost came to regret the Betws-y-Coed victory when it came to citizenship. Our draft document was balanced, particularly in the area of 'rights' and 'duties'. Citizens have both, but the left are keen on 'getting your rights' and the right stronger on duties to the state. John McGregor had replaced Baker by the time we were summoned to the Home Office to hear their views. The Home Secretary was the abrasive David Waddington, later to be seen strutting like a peacock in cocked hat and feathers as governor of the Bahamas. At his side sat

John Patten, the less illustrious of the two unrelated Pattens, and later to become a less than successful education secretary, mercifully after my time.

As those in the prison service, and police and even judges have come to learn, the Home Office does not mess around consulting folks. Waddington laid down how it was to be — bags of duties, precious few rights. McGregor, reticent at the best of times, left it to me to explain that we didn't quite work that way, that children should make up their own minds. I could see in Waddington's eyes a far from pretty look. I began to wonder how far downhill we were to go. Totalitarian states dictate what children should be taught, democracies do not.

Waddington turned to Patten for his comments. After a cringing support of Waddington's views, he complained about the lack of prominence given to car theft in our document! So much for a grand vision of education. I rejected his suggestion that the Home Office should draft five pages on their views on crime. I think that if you have ever come across a copy of the curriculum paper on citizenship you will feel reassured. On the way out, Patten took my deputy, Peter Watkins, aside and suggested that they have dinner together and see how they could get round that awkward bastard Graham! He picked the wrong man in Peter, but amply demonstrated the lack of sensitivity which was to endear him to teachers a couple of years later. The only concession we made to the right wing in the end was to put the section on duties before the section on rights.

Fortunately not all the politicians I came across were as ghastly as Waddington and Patton. Baroness Faithfull (yes, she was related to Marianne Faithfull the 1960s pop singer and actress) invited me to address the House of Lords education group, an event which turned out to be both memorable and delightful. We took tea in the Lords tearoom, magically held in a 1920s time warp, with scurrying waitresses in black with white aprons and lace caps, linen-covered tables groaning with the weight of cucumber sandwiches, scones, teacakes, stands of iced French cakes and, above all, the enticing aroma of hot buttered muffins. The Baroness recommended the muffins in particular — 'poor dears in the Commons would kill for these, but we seldom let them in.' As we munched ours in shared delight, a sort of who's who of former greats passed before our table, from prime ministers to archbishops. With some reluctance I made my way to a gloomy committee room, all heavy wallpaper, dark wood and oil paintings where a dozen or so ancient worthies awaited us with as close to eager expectancy as octogenarians can muster. After I had said my piece, I was asked some decidedly distrait questions by an aged peeress who aimed at me the only ear-trumpet I have ever come across in actual use. As I was idly speculating how a conversation between her and Mary Macrae, the eccentric vineyard owner from Suffolk might go, Baroness Faithfull leant towards me and in a stage-whispered attempt to explain the background said to me, 'Poor dear, father 86 when she was conceived, sister even worse — father 90 when she was born.' Presumably that explained everything.

The Pain Grows

ON 25th July, 1989, Kenneth Baker was summoned to the presence and informed that he had been accorded the dubious privilege of becoming Conservative Party Chairman. Refusal was out of the question and a promising career as education secretary came to a premature end. He was accused of leaving all his posts just before the attainment targets hit the fan, but in my view this was unfair. He had just about mastered the basket of writhing snakes which the DES had become, and had absorbed enough of the intricacies of education to rumble both educationists with prejudices to peddle, and officials with nests to feather. Sadly the qualities of loyalty he had shown to the cause of reform were in due course applied to keeping Margaret Thatcher in office and were to do his reputation considerable damage. His denials that anything was amiss while the Howe-led gang 'got' her are epics of hilarious lunacy. I have kept some of them on video tape and look at them whenever party chairmen tell us that the loss of 1,000 local government seats is but a triumph in disguise. I have to get the tape out quite frequently!

I had met his successor John McGregor in my Suffolk days. A fellow Scot, he represented a Norfolk constituency and was well-liked as a person. He had found 'extra' resources for computers for Suffolk, which he revealed dramatically to council leaders at a lunch in Belstead House. The leaking of his briefing notes beforehand somewhat lessened the impact, but we all simulated surprise and joy. After a spell in the treasury, to his unconcealed surprise he was catapulted into the education hot seat. I formed the impression that he had been kicked one rung too high up the greasy pole. He looked out of his depth from the start — a rabbit frightened of right-wing foxes. He was to learn that rabbits which pander to foxes have a limited life expectancy.

Baker had been accused of going too far too fast, with some justification. McGregor decided to slow the pace and try to reassure teachers by reducing the number of initiatives coming up. As I mentioned earlier, he chose to drop the scheme for teacher appraisal at the historic point where it had been accepted by all the teacher unions and local authorities. His excuse of lack of resources (it would have cost 0.4% of the teachers salaries bill) was a bad omen for future battles with the treasury. At my first meeting with him at Elizabeth House, which should have been about the national curriculum, I made an unavailing attempt to change his mind.

Apart from appraisal, we got on well and my advice was respected. Tension arose when what I said conflicted with right-wing dogma. He began to look like a man on the rack being stretched agonisingly between his head and a stranglehold on his more sensitive parts. At times he actually looked as if he was in agony. He had inherited from Baker two really hot potatoes in the shape of the working groups on history and geography both of which had strong-willed chairmen, ill-disposed to political convenience.

Baker and I had always seen history as the rock upon which the whole enterprise could founder. Quite apart from its political profile, the subject was as riven as mathematics had been. In this case, it was between the 'history is facts' school of thought — the dates, kings and battles brigade, and the 'empathy' enthusiasts. The latter believed children had to 'feel' for history — had to imagine they were living through events — chucking tea into Boston Harbour, carting corpses around in the Great Plague, or napalming peasants in Vietnam. In this setting many historians felt that history had lost its backbone, with grandfather's recollections being more important than what actually happened in the war. One can see the dangers, but as usual there was a lack of balance. The empathisers were cavalier about the need for a chronological framework or tiresome details. There were merits in both traditional and modern methods, and there should have been room for compromise, but historians do not like to compromise. None of the leading figures seemed to care much about educating children. It was tables and grammar all over again.

Much graver were the political overtones. A national curriculum in any subject implies inclusion and exclusion of material. In history the dangers are exacerbated by fears of indoctrination by selection. As an erstwhile historian myself, I had been brought up in the Glasgow school of the 1950s, influenced by giants such as Stone, James, Chandaman and Brown. Objectivity, they drummed into us, was the most essential attribute in a historian, however unattainable it might prove to be in practice. Thus one must not judge for example the massacre of Glencoe by our standards, but against the customs of the time when a spot of mass liquidation was not uncommon in Britain. At the other extreme was the fascist approach — 'doctored' history with prescribed textbooks containing the 'approved' version. My fear and that of civil servants and initially ministers too was that a preference could become a peccadillo and in time a prejudice. It needn't be and wasn't Baker's, nor McGregor's prejudice but it could be Margaret Thatcher's, and it was.

There was a feeling, not without foundation, that children had lost their pride in being British and that this could be restored by putting the 'right' interpretation on events, and selecting the events which showed the UK in the best light. But whose idea of the best light? Harking back to a 'Golden Age' is tempting but misleading. Worse still, the prime minister was, you will recall, just a trace anti-European, sowing the seeds from which today's little Englanders have sprung. She and her supporters were to demand less emphasis on European and world history and more on our own — the 'we are the best in the world' syndrome. I have some sympathy with the need to restore national pride, none with twisting history to achieve it. The study of history should encourage youngsters to study the facts, think for themselves, and form valid balanced conclusions.

Baker's choice of chairman for the history group was gloriously eccentric, Michael Saunders-Watson, a retired naval officer, whose stately home, Rockingham Castle, had a wing devoted to education for visiting school parties. Baker had met Michael at a party in Washington. Thatcher approved him unquestioningly as coming from the right background, aristocracy, discipline, sound attitudes. His credentials seemed impeccable. She was gloriously wrong. He turned out to be his own man, listened to both sides of an argument, and made decisions based on the novel premise that the interest of pupils came first. He was to the right-wingers very much 'a loose cannon'. Desperate but unavailing efforts were made to 'turn' him before it was too late.

It was realised, rightly, that he could be contaminated by dangerous lefties like me. We were not so much forbidden to meet as carefully segregated. Michael was assigned two minders — a 'trad' civil servant and an old-guard HMI, to influence him and to make sure he did not come to York. Of course he did, and while we passed up the queue selecting vol-au-vents, coleslaw and cold ham for lunch, we established contacts with side of the mouth whispers and found we were thinking on the same lines. After lunch we announced we were withdrawing alone for talks. I'll never forget the civil servant's panic. She phoned London, and came back to tell us that 'the minister forbade us to talk.' She forgot that McGregor was in the USA that day! Farce can conceal madness which in turn can mask the sinister.

As with Baker in Wales, Michael — the most delightful, urbane and civilised of men — and I met well away from York and London. Lunch at Rockingham Castle was a sheer delight, both Michael and his wife revealing a greater sympathy with the needs of children than that of civil servants and learned historians. I recall another meeting at the stables in Culzean Castle in Ayrshire where Michael was hosting a conference. He solved the 'minder' problem by assigning his two bodyguards who'd come all the way from London at taxpayers' expense to the farthest end of a 40ft-long table! They were 'below the salt' with a vengeance.

Sometimes I wonder if Baker was well aware of just whom he had chosen. Saunders-Watson was a sore disappointment to the Tory right, but in time a hero to teachers and to education. When his group's report was submitted to McGregor it was balanced, practical and sane. This put poor McGregor right behind the eight ball. He took the only way out and sat on the report for months on end. Thatcher was furious. Leaks claimed that Saunders-Watson had gone native and his group had let the nation down. She dug her toes in — facts and her facts or nothing. Crisis loomed. Saunders-Watson in the face of threats, possibly even bribes, remained calm and unmoved. Once again the national curriculum hung by a thread.

What we needed was a solution straight from the script of *Yes, Minister* — and we got it. McGregor would conduct his own investigation into history — as if the one he had had from his group was not just that! Civil servants hoped that, given time, a fudge could be achieved without outright rejection by the prime minister. Michael's group were saying openly that school history was in danger of being used as Tory propaganda — 'governments of one hue or another will try to subvert it for the purpose of indoctrination or social engineering.' Quite! Saunders-Watson defended his report stoutly. Mrs Thatcher would have none of it, but was persuaded (just) to allow the McGregor study. Jack Straw, the Labour Shadow Secretary accused her of having failed to 'pack' the working group, and now turning her back on them. The rest of us were agog to find out who would actually do the work now required: McGregor himself? Civil Servants? HMI? In the end it was done, unheralded and unappreciated, by myself and my history guru at the NCC, Nick Tate. We at least saved McGregor's bacon — he was replaced by Kenneth Clarke a few days before the mark II report was published. Although I say it myself, it was a little gem — true to Saunders-Watson, but with some 'magic words' to appease the right. Margaret Thatcher to our relief, seemed to have lost interest in pushing it farther.

I relaxed and breathed a sigh of relief. What a mistake that was. Clarke decided that history should stop in 1945 as far as schools were concerned — not in 1990 as the group had envisaged. We gleaned that history teachers were long-haired lefties to a man (and woman) and could not be trusted to put recent history fairly to pupils. Apart from the fact that history teachers in my experience tend to the dull rather than the revolutionary, it was (too much) to imagine that Clarke wanted any approach which was not biased in favour of his own party!

Apparently there then ensued with Clarke and some courageous civil servants a Dutch auction, in which Clarke started at 1945, and the others at 1990. At one point Clarke is alleged to have said he was willing to have Kruschev in but 'not that bugger Kennedy'. While the Berlin Wall crumbled, kids were to be denied the dénouement of the Communist experiment in Russia. In the end Clarke ruled history had to cease 20 years before the year in which lessons are taught. All this on the whim of one strong-minded minister, without the slightest recourse to the views of Parliament or anybody else. How far are we from executive dictatorship in the so-called cradle of democracy? This was the first major political intrusion into what is taught in the country's schools. By the way, he did ask me, jocularly I think, to exclude Palmerston (or was it Peel?) from English 19th-century history because he had not liked him at school!

Geography was no bed of roses for McGregor, either. The battleground here was old style 'capes and bays' against economic, and political geography — 'facts versus opinions' as one observer summed it up. The environment was a dicey subject too — ministers seemed to fear a generation growing up which might force them to take conservation and pollution seriously, and that sounded expensive. The group was led by Sir Leslie Fielding, a former diplomat, now Vice-chancellor of Sussex University, a tough cookie who presided at meetings in his shirt sleeves and a pair of magnificent red braces. As a diplomat, he came close to satisfying political aspirations for facts — rivers and mountains off by heart — but not near enough. He satisfied McGregor but not Clarke on whose desk his final report landed. We got more facts and less room for opinion. No assistance was to be gratuitously given to the 'green' lobby.

In the course of all this there was the inevitable incident of pure farce. The group produced no less than seven attainment targets for geography — an awful lot for children and teachers to cope with compared to three in history for example. Before I could speak to him McGregor accepted all seven. I advised him that in fact the seven could easily be reduced to three as some of them were really sub-sections of others — for example 'the home area, the UK, the world' were really only 'places'. McGregor seemed pleased until he consulted heaven knows whom, and told me that it was politically impossible to move from seven to three, but he could do a deal on five! Never have I felt so far from reality. Seven was too many but teachable in schools. Three was better in terms of workload and simplicity. There was no educational or geographical reason for five. You've guessed it. He dug his dainty little toes in, and schools were faced with five which we cobbled together to keep him happy. We could have trimmed the detailed statements from 269 to 170 to the relief of teachers and pupils alike. We did a deal for no other reason that I could see but his stubbornness on 211.

Similar shenanigans occurred over music and PE. In order to stress knowledge (right-wing) above skills (left-wing) we got close to giving more marks for knowing the theory of how to play the viola or the bagpipes than to actually performing on them. In PE a knowledge of how exercise affected circulation was more highly valued than circling the track for a few laps. Perhaps our poor Olympic performances of late are due to the weight of knowledge our athletes have to carry round the track with them. We had to cut out the compulsory learning to swim in case it cost too much — better drown a few kids in a sea-girt island than build a new pool here and there. The chairman of the PE group was Ian Beer, Headmaster of Harrow, and his group included Justin Fashanu, the footballer, who gave up after attending just one meeting. Ian could not resist telling me, in unnecessary detail I felt, how he had scored the winning try against Scotland at Twickenham in 1954 thus depriving us of the Triple Crown. My accidental revenge was to give him lunch at the Caledonian Club on the very day they unveiled a collage painting of the Scots' Grand Slam triumph of 1990. Perhaps it was he who sent me anonymously a reproduction of the painting which to this day adorns our hall in Appleby.

Both Ian Beer and Sir John Manduell, the music chairman, defended their corners vigorously. Their ultimate reward was to have their subjects made non-compulsory by Clarke — surely a philistine despite his weakness for jazz. Even the calculated inclusion of Fats Waller and Duke Ellington in a list of recommended musicians ranging from Bach to McCartney failed to win him over. The wrath of professional musicians was best expressed by Sir Simon Rattle, the conductor, who said that an over-concentration on classical music, and on listening rather than playing, would turn children off music. Clarke responded that Rattle had not read the report. In a brilliant and devastating discourse on BBC2's *The Late Show* Rattle revealed a knowledge of it far greater than Clarke's, but to no avail. So much for a balanced education.

As the storm clouds gathered round McGregor and the right-wing clamour rose to a new pitch, he became understandably touchy. Michael Fallon and Tim Eggar had been drafted in by the prime minister as junior ministers to keep an eye on him. Fallon was always there to deal with any backsliding by the secretary of state — what an atmosphere to live in within the same party. For me the difficulty was that in seeing one of the henchmen, I could not be sure sure that my views would reach McGregor, even in a distorted form.

In the midst of all this, I happened to address the Secondary Head Teachers' Association annual conference where a mischievous reporter interpreted my speech as an attack on the government — an occupational hazard by that time. McGregor was informed, flew into a rage and rang me on my car phone on the way back to York, expressing some forthright and somewhat ungentlemanly views. After he had exhausted his tirade, I said 'How about reading the speech before you comment further?' He did and to his great credit, apologised handsomely and without rancour. We spent some time on the phone that evening concocting a press release to defuse the situation in the first editions. When he left education he wrote saying how much he had appreciated my objective advice. He could have done with some more of it before he started to privatise the railways.

The succession of Kenneth Clarke spelled the end of any kind of partnership or even dialogue with professionals such as myself. Fresh from health where he had sorted out doctors and nurses, he was more than ready for teachers. The national curriculum which his own government had created was now suddenly all wrong, too complex and guess whose fault it all was? It was the old old story. For impatient politicians it has to be quick and easy. In reality life is not like that, as any parent of a teenage pupil will readily confirm. In simplifying, Clarke and his successors have opened the door wide once more to the skimping teacher, the corner cutter. Good teachers will do as they have always done. Others will again be able to sell their pupils short.

From the start, accompanied inevitably by Fallon and Eggar, Clarke met myself, the chief HMI, and the chairman of the Exam Board only after a briefing by political advisers, and made it very clear that we were there on sufferance; a tendency to sit with their feet on the table reading newspapers while we were talking, gave us a clear message. Even clearer was the hint that the NCC had had its day. Baker had once told me it had been set up to act as a safeguard against unscrupulous ministers in the future (no doubt he meant Labour ones!). But annoying bulwarks with tiresome views based on the real world and the real needs of children can be removed. Stories appeared in the press that Clarke intended to abolish NCC and SEAC. Clarke denied them, not least at a convivial dinner in a London restaurant where, accompanied by his adviser Tessa Keswick, we dined well, coped with an excellent wine and discussed jazz. He all but confessed that he believed in what I believed in but would happily go the other way to curry right-wing favour with a view to one day becoming prime minister. So far, as I write, he has failed. His genuinely liberal views, not least on Europe, have seen him slide from contender to also-ran. I admire him for holding to his beliefs now — pity he didn't do so earlier.

It was time for me to go. I had achieved most of what I reckoned I could achieve. As events were to prove and costly blunders to demonstrate, professional advice was no longer needed or desired. I could not go on justifying what I did not believe in. After amicable discussions and with handsome public tributes from Clarke, I left in the summer of 1991. I have not regretted it for one minute. Others who stayed have only succeeded in compromising their own reputations.

CHAPTER TWENTY-FOUR

Ringside Seat

On my last day of full-time employment, after visiting Elizabeth House, I had lunch aboard the *Queen Mary* — the one moored at the Embankment. It was literally where I came in, and only a few days short of 32 years since I had last had lunch in the same dining saloon somewhere between Dunoon and Rothesay in the Firth of Clyde on my last day as junior purser. Much of an age, my favourite Clyde steamer and I had both changed a bit since then — now we were both semi-retired.

In the years since my departure events in education have gone on much as before. If anything even less attention has been paid to children and their parents, although paradoxically the latter appear to have been more closely involved and consulted. Politicians have spoken feelingly of choice, have empowered parents on governing bodies and have then gone on blithely to ignore their views. I have spoken to countless parents in recent years. Their agenda remains predictable. They worry about class sizes, finding good teachers, and having adequate supplies of textbooks. They would like schools to be free of leaking roofs and to get the odd lick of paint. Politicians bang on about grant-maintained status, league tables, and choice — but they don't say whose! A grammar school in every town is hardly a clarion call to answer the challenge of education in the 21st century.

The pace of change has increased, and much of it has been frenetic rather than constructive. Change could have been justifiable if well-prepared innovations had emerged to replace shattered institutions. Instead we have created a number of 'black holes' which have yet to be filled. The spending per capita on each pupil has declined in real terms, with the result that class sizes have drifted back to where they were in the 1960s, and with woefully inadequate capital spending, school facilities, like most of the nation's infrastructure, are in a bad way. I fear that too many of our leaders see education as a burden rather than an investment. We know, even if they don't, that you cannot have both low taxes and high-quality services. Thank goodness parents and teachers have come more closely together to make the best of a bewildering situation.

And it is bewildering because the roles of professionals and laymen seem to have been transposed. Laymen now head the quangos which have succeeded the NCC and pronounce like experts — imagine our horror if an industrialist pontificated on the intricacies of brain surgery! Even more worryingly, such professionals as are left play politics in the guise of professional judgement. The integrity of Her Majesty's Inspectorate is gone — replaced by Ofsted whose chief has claimed that big classes are good for primary children (a quarter of them now on the 40 mark). Need I say more? Civil servants, once a model of impartiality envied by the world, now mouth the nostrums of their ministers, some of them defending the indefensible with visible enthusiasm instead of disowning it with haughty reserve. The traditional partnership built up over a hundred years between minister and civil servant, council chairman and chief officer has been shattered, but not replaced. There are more Clarkes and Howards than Bakers and Josephs in positions of power. Until that balance is restored, the machinery is lacking to test political ideas for practicality before letting them loose. As a result children will be even more exposed as guinea pigs.

One of the 'black holes' is in the administration of education and it is much deeper in England than in Scotland. In the south LEAs have been so weakened that there is in effect no intermediary between the whims of Whitehall and the desk of the head teacher — no one for schools and pupils to turn to for advice and support. Some might think that this does not matter overmuch; I tend to feel that somewhere between the centre and 25,000 schools there should be support and quality assurance at the least. None of our competitor nations has even contemplated opening up such a void. Indeed the trend elsewhere is to devolve decision-making to regional and local level. Abroad, one does not sense the same loss of trust between politician and professional, nor the relentless attack on public service as an ideal.

The results are all too obvious. There is no attempt to measure educational needs over an area or district. Popular schools, often in inadequate buildings, bulge at the seams; others languish in neglect, and with them their unfortunate inhabitants. Many pupils cannot get into their local schools, and no one else seems to want them. Choice has turned out to be for schools and not for pupils. One parent's choice is another's strait-jacket. Social inequalities have grown immeasurably again in recent years — as each year passes it is increasingly better to be born with a silver spoon in your mouth. The Victorian phrase 'the undeserving poor' is to be heard again in the land. While no one wishes to go back to the days of over-prescriptive local authorities with rigid control and 'catchment areas' which precluded any choice at all, we need badly to find a body (directly elected and not a quango) to represent the views of parents and to act as a court of appeal against the ever more arbitrary decisions of individual schools. The power to exclude pupils, justifiable in cases of extreme bad behaviour, is now too often used to get rid of those whose faces don't quite fit, or whose performance might not help to boost exam results. In 1995 alone, more than 12,000 were 'permanently' excluded with nowhere to go. Can that be right?

The biggest irony of all is that there is now no adequate means of ensuring the quality and standards which are the common concern of the nation. In Scotland, once again indisputably the superior system, there are still local authorities with sufficient advisers and inspectors to buttress the work of an independent HMI. In England this is no longer so and we have in its place a system of four (soon to be six) yearly inspections carried out by private inspectors under contract and of widely varying experience and quality. There is no follow-up to ensure improvement, except in the case of 'failing schools' which are beaten with a big stick although management by abuse seldom works.

The results are all too predictable. Schools devote more energy to pulling the wool over the inspectors' eyes than they do to teaching their pupils. Dressing up reports selectively for the press has become an art form. Little is done to address the twin and constant evils in our education system — low expectations and complacency. The better the pupil intake the more is this true. The leafy-suburb school with a 45% success rate at GCSE which should be 75% is selling pupils just as short as a struggling inner-city comprehensive. A visit I paid to the emergent nations of the Far East and to Hong Kong re-reinforced that point forcibly for me. We expect too little from our pupils, we settle too easily for mediocrity.

I believe the answer lies in encouraging schools to strive for national standards awards, to be gained by self-improvement set against external criteria. The reward would be accreditation to deliver a national curriculum, and even examine pupils for national certificates. Who knows the abilities of pupils better than their own teachers? Such a system has more in common with quality assurance in industry, the services, and in other countries than the quadrennial descent by a bunch of superannuated inspectors augmenting their pensions without risking the hassle of upsetting anyone! As things stand, the more governments bang on about standards, the less they do to promote them. A word of praise for teachers might not come amiss too; it would help if they praised four out of five teachers for their achievements, rather than castigating one out of five for failure. It would be nice to think that a change of government might help, but both major parties seem to have had an 'idealism bypass'. The higher they appear to put education on the agenda, the less they appear to want to spend on it. It's easier to rearrange the desks than to plug the leaks in the SS *Titanic*.

The English national curriculum might just have provided the answer to some of the questions. It could have raised expectations; it could have challenged the complacent. It could have removed the 'patchiness' of which ministers justifiably complained in the 1980s. It could have been the basis of an entitlement for every five-year-old facing compulsory schooling. With its ten subjects within a broader framework it might have answered the question of what state education is for. It might have ensured, ironically, that the basics so beloved of the right wingers were there for every pupil to the age of 16. In its infancy the national curriculum was over-prescriptive, but there was a wide consensus about its content. In any case, tactically it is easier to draw back in a calculated way, than to add material later.

The national curriculum could at least have given England a curriculum no longer the narrowest in Europe. At last it might even have given England the edge over Scotland. Scotland's unwritten national curriculum briefly looked a bit suspect in comparison — too much consensus, too little challenging debate. But it proved to have been built on firmer foundations. It is in the European and world mainstream; it has survived the onslaught.

As if frightened by the magnitude of impending success, the English establishment drew back even before it had arrived. Even before the most basic research on its effectiveness, wholesale retreat was in full swing. The whole thing was admirably summarised recently in a *Times* leader which proclaimed: 'At last we have pared the national curriculum to the basics of literacy and numeracy.' Doesn't that say it all? We've marched them up to the top of the hill and we've marched them down again. Who cares about the children?